# HIGHER EDUCATION TODAY AND TOMORROW

# HIGHER EDUCATION
## TODAY AND TOMORROW

UMRAO SINGH CHAUDHARI

GYAN

Higher Education Today and Tomorrow

Rs. 750



ISBN: 978-81-212-1018-8



Published in 2009 in India by
Gyan Publishing House
23, Main Ansari Road, Darya Ganj,
New Delhi-110002
Phones : 23282060, 23261060
Fax : 011-23285914
E-mail: books@gyanbooks.com
Website: www.gyanbooks.com

*Lasser Type Setting by*: Rudra Computer Graphics, Delhi
*Printed at* : G. Print Process, Delhi-35

# Contents

# Preface

In the pages of this book the author presents a critical analysis of different aspects of the higher education. He also puts forth valuable suggestions to unknot the problems generally faced by the administrators, teachers and the students in an educational setting. A special feature of the book is the inclusion of the chapters on the Indian mind; culture, development and globalization, and Hinduism and its relevance in global academic scenario. These topics will help the readers to develop an Indian perspective on higher education. To relate higher education to contemporary social issues, themes of social justice and excellence; human rights education, peace education, social change and education, spiritual leadership and value orientation in higher education have been included, besides main stream higher education topics.

It is very often heard, seen and felt that only change is permanent and uncertainty is certain in today's world. Social change has become a powerful determinant of our educational thinking and doing. We, therefore, need to have different epistemology and pedagogy for the institutions of higher learning. Growing complexity of the world has the potential to dislocate the 'self. Therapeutic pedagogy helps restoration of an identity between the 'self' and meanings .What matters is not knowledge that teachers impart to the learners, because knowledge and ideas are mostly short-lived and contestable. On the other side students' 'mode of being' that enables them to deal with super complex world, is of the utmost importance for copability. We are, therefore required to deemphasise or displace knowledge from the core of our pedagogies. The student's being has to take the centre stage.

A general feeling resonates in this work is that the indifference, thick skinned consciousness and connivance of governments ( central and state), apex organisations like the UGS, AICTE, and NCTE and professoriate of colleges and universities has led to the present downturn and stagnation of higher education in the country. It is a truism to say that no understanding of the academic disease is possible without the understanding of the academic man. The author of this book believes that recovery of disastered higher education is possible through the sincere efforts of the professoriate.

It should, therefore, be our first priority to make the professional preparation of college and university teachers much more effective and relevant to the demands of the changing times. Professors ought to be people, put on perfection, bubbling with excitement for ideas. The faculty should be a band of creative scholars stimulating each other, and freely determining curricular activities by involving the learners.

Classrooms of our colleges and universities have been reduced to dull "lesson hearing rooms". They are 'antidialogical' and suffers form 'narration sickness'. They ought to be made hospitable to questioning and disagreements. The whole art in the organization of a university is the provision of a faculty whose learning is lighted up with imagination and who can induce students in imaginative acquisition of knowledge. This variety of teachers or edupreneurs can transform a university into a 'testing track' of competitive and dissenting ideas. For successful higher education there must always be certain freshness in knowledge dealt with. It must either be new in itself or it must be invested with some novelty of application to the new world or the new times. We are living in an epistemic and inquiring society wherein knowledge, meaning and truth are not given.

They have to be explored and constructed in an interactive and collaborative endeavour

of the university teachers and students. Yesterday is not good enough for tomorrow. Today's universities are not good enough for the new globalizing world. Xhey must take the new "Avatar" to be 'entrepreneurial' universities to know how and to what extent it might be possible to think differently instead of endorsing what is already known. A blend of values, attitudes and assumptions, a certain moral tone, a special quality of imagination, a particular flavour of sensibility are the indestructive electrons that constitute the nucleus of the soul of our universities.

In the end, I would like to express my grategulness to the scholars whose ideas or views referred in this work.

**Prof. U.S. Chaudhari**

# Introduction

## An Epistemology and Pedagogy for Uncertainty

People dislike education, because it is not presented to them in their youth for what it is. It is made a painful experience to them by burdening their minds with accumulated facts and technical details. Renowned historian and philosopher Will Durant points out that education is not imparted to the youth "as an ennobling intimacy with great men." He insists in his book: *The Pleasures of Philosophy* that education should be considered not as the preparation of the individual to "make a living", but as the development of every potential capacity in him for the comprehension, control and appreciation of his world. "Above all", says Durant (1957), "education in its fullest definition is the technique of transmitting as completely as possible, to as many as possible, that technological, intellectual, moral and artistic heritage through which the race forms the growing individual and makes him human. Education is the reason why we behave like human beings".

Education has, above all, an impact on society as a whole. It produces learning communities not just learned individuals. Beyond private returns, education produces social returns. By producing both learned individuals and learned communities, education produces entrepreneurial individuals and entrepreneurial environments. The enterprise of higher education endeavours to facilitate the 'Ascent of Man' by equipping the youth with right and recent knowledge, skill and attitude. It prepares youth for ensuring peaceful and creative solution of problems and resolution of conflicts by resorting to the methods of dialogue and discussions.

"Human history", writes H.G. Wells, "is a race between education and catastrophe". I think, history is also a war between mediocrity and genius. It is known to us that in the days of rapid social change, rate of catastrophic occurrences get increased in the society.

Educational studies have revealed that the nation is at risk due to the rising tide of mediocrity. We must, therefore, make higher education sufficiently efficient and effective to preclude and prevent the occurrence of mediocrity and catastrophe in the country. At the same time, paramountcy of knowledge has been recognized as the major characteristic of the new age or the third millennium. Knowledge or cognitive component is increasing in almost all the jobs and occupations. This development has led to the idea of a 'knowledge society' and knowledge-driven economy. Innovativeness and research have assumed greater importance in the institutions of higher learning. Quality, morality, creativity and professionalism (or training) have come to be known as the special features of the 21st century. Consequently, higher education has become a condition of survival and capability all over the world.

Universities, though facing marginalization, are indeed in transition. They are struggling to reborn in a new *Awatar* that will strike a balance between traditional academic culture and market culture. The world needs the university more than ever, but in the form of a revised and reconceptualized edition. The university will continue to create an autonomous space (or structure) for debate between expert and lay cultures. It will enable society to live with choice and uncertainty. Taming (or humanizing) the new technologies and providing a cultural orientations for society will be another task of the university to be undertaken in near future. For these and some other reasons that may surface in course of time, the university has a continued relevance.

Fear and suspicion have been expressed by the academics about the risk involved in the market oriented model of higher education. Marketization is seen as possibly leading to moral risk, profit-seeking, unfair competitions, brokering, bargaining, academic capitalism and managerialism. It is also feared that a market-driven higher education system will produce 'barbarians', whose expertise is usable, specific and vendible, but not sophisticated. The university may be fashioned into "a shopping mall, a degree mill and a patent factory" with short-sighted profit-making as a common denominator. Many quarters, however, emphasize the fact that interactive teaching, unfettered research and pursuit of truth must remain the primary and most important task of universities, and reform should support it. Reforms should not be made for the university but they ought to be initiated in the university since it still remains the 'conscience' of the society.

It is perhaps very difficult to implant, truly permanent changes, in the university culture without doing deep reaching longitudinal studies. Infact, reasonable market orientation in higher education is not meant to supercede academic practices but instead to adapt these practices to suit entrepreneurial activity. Institutional practices are more permanent and change more difficult than the discourse which advocates the 'entrepreneurial university' would lead us to believe. The idea of 'entrepreneurial university', advanced by Burton R. Clark (1998), emphasizes more strongly than the 'innovative university' concept, the conscious measures to be taken to bring about changes in the attitudes of the organization.

It is very often said that only change is permanent and uncertainty is certain in today's world. Accelerated change confounds and makes the situation exceedingly complex. People confronts conceptual chaos and emotional insecurity. Growing super complexity of the world is characterized by four concepts, namely, contestability, challengeability, uncertainty and unpredictability. Complexity is defined as that state of affair in which the demands before an individual exceed the resources available to meet them. Consequently, one is faced with an overload of data and entities. Such conditions generate challenge and even stress. The meta concept of super complexity is an outcome of proliferation of multiplicity of knowledges leading to a conceptual overload and plurality of knowledge frameworks or approaches to understanding. An individual finds it difficult to make a choice for a particular framework out of the rival and problematic many. For shifting the university's knowledge creation function from an 'endorsing machine' to one that seeks to produce radically new or different frame of understanding would require significant change in the ways of conducting research, in devising new reward structures that encourage creative effort, and in forming of multidisciplinary groupings.

According to Ronald Barnett (2000), in an age of super complexity, the university needs nothing less than an epistemology for uncertainty. This epistemology for the university is open, bold, engaging and accessible. It can have at least the following four elements:

1. The capacity for revolutionary reframing;
2. The capacity for critical interrogation of all claimants for knowledge and understanding;
3. The capacity for enabling individual to feel at ease in an uncertain world; and
4. The capacity for developing powers of critical action. *

In a world of supercomplexity, there can be no firmness or surety to the epistemological base of the university because knowledge has limited shelf-life and it is not beyond scrutiny

* Barnett, Ronald (2000) 'University knowledge in an Age of Super-complexity'. *Higher Education*, 40 : 409-422.

However, in adopting such a novel epistemology, the university would regain continuity with its rhetorical past, and its earlier belief in itself as a site for enlightenment and cognitive struggle.

It has also been pointed out by Barnett that in an age of radical uncertainly, the key educational challenge is not one of knowledge as such. It is that of 'being'. If any account of the world is contestable and if our sense of 'who we are' and our relationships to each other and to the world are insecure; 'being' overtakes knowledge as the key epistemological concept. Teaching and learning in this situation must take the form of a 'therapeutic pedagogy', which deals with the students' experience and his human being as such. It allows for the discharge of repressed claims and offers rooms for personal engagement and negotiation with proliferating and contestable frames of meaning, which is normally denied in institutions and media.

Super complexity dislocates the self. Therapeutic pedagogy helps restoration of an identity between self and meanings. It does so by allowing space for meaning to come from within a person. "A therapeutic pedagogy offers a chance of recovering the self. It looks back to that which was suppressed but also looks forward to new realization of human beings" Thus, in these times of change and uncertainly, the university is required to have a mission of enabling youth to act purposefully with a sense of direction. Unless those action-based epistemologies are coupled with the university's functions, sheer technicism will result. After all, the modem world needs not just competent teachers but teachers who can question their own actions, and who are capable of envisaging a novel form of professionalism. As academics, university professors should never lose sight of their obligation to create new futures, to inspire students to ask divergent and impossible questions, to think of unthinkable and to come out of current boundaries and frameworks of typical knowledge.

Barnett wants that teaching should be directed "to create epistemological and ontological disturbance in the minds and in the 'being' of students...... A genuine higher learning is apparent when the student is enabled to understand the contestability of all the frameworks that he or she encounters and comprehends, and to confront that contestability in all its presenting forms". This of course needs a different approach and pedagogy which gives students space to develop their voice. Infact, in these days of upheavals and disorientations, what matters is not the knowledge, that teachers impart to the learners, because knowledge and ideas are mostly short-lived and contestable, but student's 'mode of being', that enables them to deal with a super complex world, is of utmost importance for copability. Hence, promotion of such personal qualities as breadth of mind, courage, self-reliance, flexibility, adaptability and capacity to present new and counter frames of understanding must get preference over communication of transient knowledge for responding uncertainty. We, therefore, need to displace knowledge from the core of our pedagogies. The student's being has to take centre stage.

# 1

# The Indian Mind

In his book *Gods and Politicians*, Bruce Grant, former High Commissioner of Australia in New Delhi, observed: "India is a place from which no traveler returns unchanged. Of the countries I know well India is the most sensual. It is the evocation of things seen, heard, touched, tasted and smelled-rather than intellectual recall, that enables me how best to remember it.... It is an experience, an idea, a word meaning, many things to many people." India is one of the few countries of the world which has a very ancient culture and civilization. It is distinctive for its antiquity and continuity. Apart from its own vitality, the continuity of India is largely due to its ability to adapt to alien ideas without losing its own identity. Her constant contact with the outside world also gave India the opportunity to contribute to other civilizations.

Every country has its own uniqueness and individuality which is mirrored in its academic, social and cultural life and pursuits. This can be termed as its "mind" or "collective consciousness" which determines attitudes and directs the gesture of its people. While India never lost sight of the necessity of the material and intellectual dimension of life, she laid a particular emphasis on the moral and spiritual aspect. This spiritual dimension was non-existent in other countries until two thousand years ago, and then it developed only as an adjunct of religious dogmatism attached to a particular prophet and his set of religious tenets.

Spiritualism in India meant a dedication of one's life to the perfection of soul or self-realization. Of all the countries of the world, India alone, with all the hypocrisy and cant attributed to it by some foreign and even Indian writers, justifiably or otherwise, allows and even encourages search and research in the spiritual field as a worthy whole time profession. The Indian philosophical tradition, from the period of Vedas upto the modern time, presents a glorious record of reflection on man's nature and his destiny. Spinoza has correctly said that "the intellectual love of God" is a summary of Hindu Philosophy.

Indian civilization is essentially religious. It is engaged in a continuous and sincere pursuit of the sacred. People of India have strong sense of individuality and at the same time, a sense of society at large, which enables them to think in terms of the common interests of groups and classes. The caste and guild system, the nightmare of all governments for their clannishness and economic power, stem from this ability to congregate. Spread over a huge geographical area 'Indianism' that is the essence of a polymorphous culture, is difficult to define. It acquires different postures and modes according to taste, attitudes and mental sets of different groups and people united by a typical acceptance of certain constant social and cultural factors, such as the caste system, the belief in the cycle of successive lives, and a sense of nationhood.

Aristotle (greater part of 4th century B.C.) had inborn contempt and prejudice for Asiatics and Indians. Ignoring Kautilya who was chronologically near and comparable to him, Aristotle used to address Asiatics as barbarians. He conceded that natives of Asia are intelligent and inventive, but they are wanting in spirit, and therefore, they are always in a state of subjection and slavery. Those who have read the accounts of early English travellers to India, came to believe that the

Hindus were like 'fiendish race' or 'a lesser breed without law'. Reputed indologists, like J.Z. Holwell. Alexander Dow, N.B Halhed, Charles Wilkins, Max Mueller, William Jones and scores of others, however, proved that such a belief was wrong. Max Mueller remarked: "If, I were asked under what human sky the human mind has most fully developed some of its choicest gifts, has most deeply pondered on the greatest problems of life, and has found solutions of some of them which will deserve the attention even of those who have studied Plato and Kant, I would point to India". Similarly, in his profound work: *The Story of Civilization, Pt-1 : Our Oriental Heritage*, Will Durant has said that "this is the India...... that patient scholarship is now opening up, like a new intellectual continent, to that Western mind which only yesterday thought civilization an exclusively European thing". Again, in the same book Durant cites a European philosopher who believed that "Indian wisdom is the profoundest that exists", and also quoted the statement of a great novelist: "I have not found in Europe or America, poets, thinkers and popular leaders equal or even comparable to those of India today". Deterioration of Indian art, culture and thought started with the decline of Gupta Period (500 A.D.), which is generally known as, the 'Golden Age' of India. Most of the energy and imagination of Indians was dissipated in maintaining the purity of their blood by imposing certain restrictions on the intermingling of the people of alien races. This attitude was (unfortunately) further reinforced by various rituals, caste consciousness and untouchability.

In medieval India, the intellectual life was embodied in the teaching of Hindu and Muslim mystic saints. Most of them denounced idolatory, caste system and untouchability. They also condemned polytheism and belived in one God. Seventeenth Century marked the period of climax of India's medieval feudal culture. At the beginning of the 18th century the Mughal structure began to crumble. The Britishers took the fullest advantage of the weakness and follies of the Indian feudal rulers - Hindu and Muslim alike. Thus, another era of oppression started from 1757 onwards.

From the last decade of medieval period to the beginning of the modem times, Indian thought is found to be in the grip of darkness. No notable progress in the realm of thinking was noticeable at this time. Political subjugation brought all round demoralization to Indians. The English education in India, as introduced by British rule, influenced the minds of educated men to a great extent. They became great admirers of every thing Western and in course of time came to develop an inferiority complex and an attitude of contempt for the great religious and cultural traditions of their own country. This was the first time, perhaps, that the Indian mind was thrown off its balance. Even the Muslim invasions and conquests had not produced a result of this kind. Indian scholars took great interest either in elaborating western concepts or in getting endorsement of their ideas in western literature. This 'dependence proneness' or 'follower syndrome' of Indians increased so much so that their own reasoning ability and creativity were blunted and stifled. As Shils (1960) has pointed out, the effectiveness and productivity of Indian intellectuals got more restricted than their capacities made it necessary.

The architects of 19th century renaissance reinterpreted the religious scriptures and made vigorous efforts at synthesizing tradition and modernity. Raja Ram Mohun Roy (1772-1833), the father of Indian recovery and perhaps the first modern man in India, powerfully pleaded that he was not opposed to 'Brahminism' in its original form, but to a perversion of it. The greatest contribution of the 20th century Indian thinkers is that they gave social content to the spiritual tradition. They took an integral and all comprehensive view of life and existence. The idealistic tradition of the West and the Christian ideal of love and social service found expression in their writings. Unlike the 19th century reformers, the 20th century thinkers have made tremendous impact on the entire

Indian Society. It is fast shading its rigidity, 'holier than thou' attitude and traditional approach to deliverance. Tagore has beautifully expressed this in his own poetic style:

"Deliverence is not for me in renunciation.

I feel the embrace of freedom in a thousand bonds of delight."

Those Indian writers who have settled abroad have, by and large, painted a dark, gloomy and negative picture of India. To V.S. Naipaul India is wounded beyond recovery. Indians have stunted ego and they are incapable of creative work. This is too pessimistic a portrayal of Indian mind. Khushwant Singh is forthright in his comment that Naipaul's book: *India - A Wounded Civilization* presents a totally negative picture of the country and the illustrations have been so chosen as to fit into his preconceived notions of India. Foreign Indian writers don't visit India for decades during which India acquires a very different landscape. Therefore, their writings remain superficial and unreal. Because of their outmoded knowledge they fail to address themselves to the major and vital issues India is facing today. India may be a wounded civilization but it has immense power of resistance and recovery.

"The utmost creed of India", says Tagore, "is to find the one in the many, unity in diversity. India does not admit difference to be a conflict, nor does she espy an enemy in every stranger. So she repels none, destroys none, and strives to find a place for all in a vast social order. She acknowledges every path and recognizes greatness whenever she finds it. Since India has this genius for unification, we do not have to fear imaginary enemies. We may look forward to our own expansion as the final result of each new struggle. Hindu and Buddhist, Muslim and Christian shall not die fighting on Indian soil. Here they will find harmony." Thus, the Indian people have an enormous sense of accommodation and assimilation.

The spirit of modern India is something like the 'spirit of nature' itself. It is ever new, constantly changing, yet old. While

Indians are actively engaged in their pursuits of scientific achievement, the *Vedas* and *Upanishadas* will continue to fascinate and inspire them. Their search for the ultimate continues without losing interest in the mundane pursuits. Meanwhile, they will bear the weight of poverty with their characteristic quietness and contentment. Mahatma Gandhi's concept of 'Ram Rajya' will always lure and inspire them more than the Marx's 'dialectical materialism.' And, perhaps, their means will be as important as their ends. Yet, what India represents today is the emergence of a new 'Sarvodaya Civilization', not merely the continuation of the old 'Varanashram Dharma'. The famous philosopher and historian Arnold Toynbee is quite reasonable in his assertion that "at this supremely dangerous moment in human history, the only way of salvation for mankind is an Indian way. Here we have the attitude and the spirit that can make it possible for human race to grow together into a single family and in this atomic age, this is the only alternative to destroying ourselves."

# 2

# Culture, Development and Globalization

Mahatma Gandhi, infact, characterized the whole of 20th Century. It is said that Italy had renaissance, Germany had reformation and France had Voltaire, who was half a revolution. Similarly India had Gandhi who was a full revolution. He was addressed as 'Mahatma' by the great poet and Noble Lauriate Rabindra Nath Tagore. In the words of Romain Rolland (1976), he was the 'christ without a cross' and 'one man army'. It was he who made the social invention of 'Satyagraha' which was termed by Martin Luther King Jr as a 'moral equivalent of war'. For him non-violence was the most desperate battle and an annunciation of peace on earth.

To begin with, Gandhi started his struggle against injustice in Africa, which inspired the oppressed and subjugated people to rise against all sorts of imperialism: mental, cultural, political, philanthropical and technological. He made it very clear in his well known small book: *Hind Swaraj* (1909) that he had no grudge against Britishers as human beings, but certainly had one against their culture which was based on exploitation, oppression, violence and injustice. The great poet and humanist Rabindra Nath Tagore wrote an immortal and emancipatory poem which harboured in tender words a lofty and irrepressible quest for the 'heaven of freedom', where the mind works without fear, the head is held high and the world is not divided by narrow domestic walls. Both Gandhi and Tagore agreed that "we must persuade the butterfly that the freedom of the sky is better than the shelter of the cocoon." Tagore's poem resounds and recaptures the Indian 'Vedic Vision' of the world: 'Vasudhaiv Kutumbkam' (that the whole earth is a human family). This great poem was though, thought and written by Tagore, it was Gandhi who really fought and struggled to translate its central idea in to practice. This cultural quest and social trend continues to get reflected and reinforced in the Indian society, culture and the polity.

**Culture**

The essence of culture is 'refinement' and that of civilization is 'civility'. Culture is mostly perceived as the personality of a society and civility as its character. Culture is "blood of blood and bone of bone" in the sense that it is fused and merged into what we call character and morale. It remains with us when all else is taken away. "Culture", says Alfred North Whitehead, is "the activity of thought and receiptiveness to beauty and humane feelings. Scraps of information have nothing to do with it. A merely well-informed man is a most useless bore on God's earth." In real culture what one is after is some new angle of vision, some new organ of research, some new mirror of reflection. A cuitured person seeks is some new avenue of approach, some unexplored secret of sensation, some fresh magnet of sensitivity that will help him/her to explore like a liberated tide certain hitherto untouched promontories (Powys, 1960). "Culture does not show itself among men", says St. Paul, "as something ponderous, majestic, pompous, imposing. It does not 'show' itself at all: Like the *Tao* so subtly described by the philosopher Kwang Tze three hundred years before christ, it flows through the air, swims in the water, burrows in the earth, moves imperceptibly from mind to mind, and 'by doing nothing does everything'. It draws out others rather than asserts itself; it is a listner rather than a disputant. It has as much respect for the peculiar intelligence of women as for the peculiar intelligence of men. It uses the woman's mind as well as the man's mind in its perception of truth."

Perhaps, like a saint or a poet, John Cowper Powys had a premonition of the spirit of the new age and new humanism of the third millennium. He says in his prophetic words that "there is no great culture needed to make one behave with courtesy and lively attention to the rich, the beautiful, the famous. Where our true sophisticated culture shows itself in our attitude to the unimportant, the negligible, the weak, the mean-spirited, the pigheaded. The weaker and sillier a person is, the more intense should be the concentration with which one listens to his words and gives his fumbling spirit one's full attention, for it always acquires more effort to get interesting reaction from a simple fool than from clever devil who delights in showing off." In fact, Mahatma Gandhi represented this true and sophisticated culture when he asserted that the meek and humble shall inherit the earth.

**Culture and Development**

Unesco in 1982 and 1998, and the World Bank in 1998 organized international conferences to highlight the interplay between culture and development. These conferences in their reports pleaded for cultural policies for nations, and also for acceptance of culture as an investment in sustainable development. Following the recommendations of the conferences, 'UN World Decade for Cultural Development' (1988-97) was organized through out the world to deliberate and to understand the impact of culture on the process of development. The World Bank has also taken an initiative to give financial assistance to such projects which treat culture as an economic resource.

Since culture is a matter of attitude, beliefs, values and discipline, it may sometime hinder and many a times help the process of development. Gunnar Myerdal (1972) in *Asian Drama* made it very clear that in the soft political system of democracy 'social discipline' is very essential for rapid development. Economic growth is not merely a matter of physical resources or of training skilled workers, it needs the education of the whole population in new ways of life, thought and work. Robert Heilbroner (1963) looks at the journey to economic development undertaken by the traditional society as the 'great ascent' and points out that the essential condition to be successful in this uphill task is a 'human change on a grand scale'. He further explicates that "The mere lay-in of a crore of capital equipment, indispensable as that is for further economic expansion, does not yet catalyse a tradition-bound society into a modern one. For that catalysis to take place, nothing short of a pervasive social transformation will suffice, a whole-sale metamorphosis of habits, a wrenching reorientation of values concerning time, status, money, work, and an un-weaving and reweaving of the fabric of daily existance itself."

In the times of rapid change, we experience an increase in uncertainty, emergency, novelty and transcience around us. This situation demands flexibility, initiative, innovativeness, adventure and creativity in all our roles and undertakings. We need to have a quick mind-shift and an experimental attitude to cope with the occurence of unanticipated and unexpected change. Alvin Toffler (1970) has rightly said that "by making imaginative use of change to channel change, we can not only spare ourselves the trauma of future shock, we can reach out and humanize distant tomorrows." Therefore, greater emphasis has to be put on imaginative consideration of happenings and knowledge, in our homes and schools, instead of making the boys and girls our robots and clones. Moulds and models have a limited use in the age of speed and spontaneity. Creativity with conscience, breakthrough-insights and proactivism are the intellectual missiles of the day to answer the questions and challenges of all the fronts of life. If 'yesterday' is too much with us, it becomes a burden not only on our memory, but also on our imagination. The past has both its value and limitation. Yesterday mind, only in very rare case can solve the problems of tomorrow. 'Continuous renewal' or 'cultural rebirth' is, therefore, the insurance of survival and advancement.

Besides equipping individuals with a change-prone frame of mind in the modern times, cultural and educational institutions should also aim at developing what A.N. Whitehead has called an 'ultimate morality of mind'. Whitehead has also named it a 'style of life'. This style of life is the last aquirement of an educated mind. It hates waste, economizes material and prefers good work. Infact, the substance of this attitude to life is almost synonymous with excellence. It is very much useful and relevant for the economies of scarcity and destitution, because it stresses judicious and parsimonious use of every thing. Thus, by adopting and assimilating Whitehead's concept of 'style of life', the increasing trend of over-consumption and wastefulness can be curbed and the scare resources can be conserved, preserved and shared.

According to Jean Dreze and Amartya Sen's (1995) analysis, poverty is a deficit of power and participation in the social, economic and political space. Various cultural forms and activities can be employed to awaken the poverty-stricken masses to the degrading subhuman conditions in which they are enveloped. To a great extent, they are suffering because they are afraid of freedom. They find more security in dependence. Their mind-set is badly under the grip of fatalism and survival-mindedness. What is urgently needed is to widen their economic horizon and to inculcate in them a taste for success and self-sufficiency through development oriented rehumanizing-communication and dialogue. By employing adult education strategies and 'Swadhyay' type enabling practices and activities the poor and the depressed can be conscientized to come out of the attitudinal prison erected around them by the circumstances of oppression and exploitation. Cultural stimulus and art forms can be employed to alleviate poverty and to stimulate the underprivileged people to come out of the mental ghettos to revolt against the unjust socio-economic system and the domesticating and coersing social forces.

To make culture a vehicle of emancipation, change and development' a national policy on culture has to be evolved. Then, adequate public and private financial assistance should be made available to design and organize variety of cultural programmes to transform the attitudes and outlook of the depressed masses, so that they themselves can organize and agitate for their empowerment and participation in the decision making process. Infact, these people have valuable indigenous wisdom and traditional knowledge which is lying dormant and supressed due to the fear psychosis created by the dominant class of the society. Even the enlightened intelligentia has distanced itself from the culturally and economically deprived masses. If truely cultured people start taking interest in the problems and helplessness of the oppressed masses, then not only these suffering men and women will be restored to their cultural capital of latent knowledge and wisdom, but the intellgentia will also be benefited and enriched experientially by entering into an interaction with them. Catalan Poet Joan Brossa's statement: "... .culture is the best weapon man has against oppression" is quite assuring and inspiring to all of us.

## Globalization vs Indigenization

Nothing imperializes like globalization and modernity. Both of these concepts are of western origin. They are eating away the very vitals of the developing countries. It is the TNCs that are glorifying globalization. Geeta Kapur (2000) has very pertinently pointed out that the "first world has entirely appropriated the term international for its own perception and exploits." The phenomenon of globalization and modernity amply demonstrates as to how world affairs are conducted according to the "hegemonic goodwill or hierarchy of economic interests" of the first world. Geeta Kapur further examines the discordant idea of globalization and observes that "the terminology of globalization refers unblushingly to an ideology of the market, dictated by the international funding agencies to a global market of which USA having 'won' the cold war, is moral conductor."*

The twins of globalization and modernity are the camouflaged forces that have been invented to dominate the non-Western world and to submerge their identity and culture in the waters of Western thought and tradition. These two concepts are largely synonymous and reinforcing to each other. Both of them are hegemonic, arbitrary and exploitative in their hidden meaning and approach. Thanks to the rise of the Tiger Economies of the four East Asian countries, that made them assertive and challenging. To begin with these countries refused to accept that Westernity and modernity are the one and the same thing. India and the Islamic countries also followed the suit to assert the superiority of their cultures and civilizations. The Asian challenge to superiority of western culture is manifest in almost all the Asian civilizations.

"European Colonialism is over", says Huntington (1997), and "American hegemony is receding. The erosion of Western culture follows, as indigenous historically rooted mores, languages, beliefs and institutions reasserted themselves. The growing power of non-Western societies produced by modernization is generating the revival of non-Western cultures through out the World." This process of indigenization is a revolt against the dominance, homogenizing and monopolizing tendency of the Western countries in the field of culture. Asian and other non-Western countries have rejected the secular, relativistic, degenerate culture associated with the West. It is a

* In her book: *When was Modernism*, refer the Chapter: 'Globalization: Navigating the Void', p. 339.

repulsion to what has been termed the "Westoxification" of non-Western societies. It is a sort of proclamation of 'Cultural independence' from the West and an assertion that the non-Western world can be 'modern' without undergoing the process of Westernization.

In Asian countries, the process of indigenization and Asianization are in progress since the year 1980. The global process of indigenization is evident broadly in the revivals of religion and cultural nationalism occuring in so many parts of the world, and most prominently in the cultural resurgence in Asian and Islamic countries encouraged largely by their 'economic and demographic dynamism'.

It is very interesting to note that 'democratization' and 'Westernization' can not go hand in hand. Huntington says that "democracy is inherently a parochializing not a cosmopolitanizing process. Politicians in non-western societies do not win elections by demonstrating how Western they are. Electoral competition instead stimulates them to fashion what they believe will be the most popular appeals, and those are usually ethnic, nationalist and religious in character". Thus, estrangement of the politician from the culture of the nation will not permit him to be a representative or a leader of the people even in a democratic system. Since democracy is the voice of the people, it must be rooted in the cultural ethos of the people. John Dewey (1966) goes a step further to say that a democracy should be generation-specific. Every generation should give birth to its own democracy afresh.

But, on the contrary, the masses or voters feel politically helpless and impotent because there is neither any platform nor the politicians available to them to listen to their ideas and problems. Toffler (1970) has very sensitively diagnosed this problem of peoples' powerlessness. "Indeed" he (Toffler) says, "nowhere in politics is there an institution through which an ordinary man can express his ideas about what the distant future ought to look, feel or taste like. He is never asked to think about this and on the rare occasions when he does, there is no organized way for him to feed his ideas into the arena of politics. Cut off from the future, he becomes a political eunach.

Infact, indigenization is an expedition for the search of a nation's identity. The values of culture provide the building blocks of identity. In the early 1990s, a relevant effort to identify commonalities in the value-spectrum of the country, the then president Wee Kim Wee took an initiative to innunciate 'shared values' of -Singaporeans as under (Huntington, 1996) :

1. Nation before (ethnic) community and society above self;
2. Family as the basic unit of society;
3. Regard and community support for the individual;
4. Consensus instead of contention;
5. Racial and religious harmony.

This set of values, it is expected, will define a Singaporean cultural identity which was shared by its ethnic and religious communities, and which distinguished it from the West. This effort in the direction of cultural nationalism substantiates John Naisbitt's (1990) observation made in context with globalization of life styles : "The more homogenous our life styles become, the more stead-fastly we shall cling to deeper values - religion, language, and literature. As our worlds grow more similar, we will increasingly treasure the traditions that spring from within...... cultural nationalism runs deep. When it is challenged, or when there is a new opportunity for its expression, it will rise to the surface."

The then Vicc-Finance Minister of Japan, Eisuke Sukakibara declared publicly in January 1999 that the current variety of globalization is unstable and unsustainable. Economics has become devoid of history and society. He cited Karl Polyani to point out that "instead of the economy being embedded in social relations, social relations are embedded in the economic system...... Markets are sustainable only in so far as they are embedded in social and political institutions which secure moral and ethical quality of our lives". Finally,

Sakakibara said that "globalization thriving amidst diversity is my vision for the next century, and I strongly believe this coexistence of diverse civilizations with global networking will create a much better world than the unilateral imposition of monolithic ideologies, such as market fundamentalism."*

A discerning Marya Mannes has made a very significant observation on the unbridled race for money and wealth, going on in the acquisitive societies. "In the race for money" she says, "some men may come first, but man comes last." Similarly, man's bosom is swelled when he sees a long list of scientific and technological achievements, but he ignores the fact, brought to the notice of scientists by Martin Luther King Jr. that "Our scientific power has outburnt our spiritual power. We have guided missiles and misguided men". We very often miss the wood for a tree. Man is not only a Homo-Economicus or a Techno sapien, he has social, aesthetic and moral dimensions too. He has responsibility towards himself, his fellow human beings, and nature. Why do we pretend to know-not that a hole has been pierced in the moral ozone by our own follies and arrogance. Seers and saints have warned us repeatedly that every success or failure is a moral success or failure. The great paradox of our age is that we have an unprecedented quantum of knowledge at our command, but we have not been able to solve the basic human problems. To know so much and to have control over nothing is a big tragedy of our times. Does it not indicate that we hardly bother to anticipate the consequences of having new knowledge, and also don't try to discipline the power of knowledge by the sense of values.

What we expressly need on the occasion of the commencement of the third millennium is the dedication for an integrated and balanced development of all the aspects of human life, not of one at the expense of the other. "Human race's

---

* 'Beyond Market Fundamentalism' by Rajni Bakshi in *The Hindu*, September 24, 2000.

prospects of survival" says Arnold Toynbee, "were considerably better when we were defenceless against tigers than we are today when we have become defenceless against ourselves."

Humanist psychologists and social scientists have been able to diagnose the human situation. They are of the opinion that the qualities of love, reason and relatedness must be restored to the human race. Some super social trends like a deepening individuality, a wider diversity, more freedom and interdependence of individuals, organizations and nations have also been identified. But, unless rapidity of change is not restrained and guided properly, it will continue to overwhelm men's physical defences, discisional processes and the quest for a coherent living.

It is quite relevant to recall, in the present context, the question raised by our former Hon'ble President Dr. K.R. Narayan about technopoly. He asks: "has the cultural development of man, of society, kept pace with the rapid and spectacular technological advance? What is emerging seems to be a new 'technological Brahminism' when the brain and automatic substitutes of the brain do increasing volume of work. Cultural pursuits are not the things occupying people liberated from drudgery, manual work and even work by their natural brain." "To support his opinion, Dr. Narayan cites Mahatma Gandhi's statement made perhaps long ago. Gandhi said "if by some chance one man could plough up the whole of land of India, control all the agricultural produce, and if millions had no other occupation, they would being idle become dunces, as many have already become. In an another illustration Gandhi pointed out that "if 30 people can produce enough for three million, he would not mind it, provided the others could be given employment and some useful work." "Technological advance", says former Dr. Narayan, "without cultural advance is posing as dangerous a situation as the misuse of technology for destructive purposes. It is producing not men with culture, enjoying arts, music and sciences but indulging in drugs, sex, violence and crime."

Then, "what is needed most today, what young people and particularly teenagers who are about to complete their secondary studies", says former Dr. Federico Mayor, Director General of Unesco, "are demanding of us, more or less explicitly, are bench-marks, compasses and navigation charts. Unless we supply them with this essential equipment without delay, we risk witnessing major upheavals, perhaps within the next five years. We must take action, even at risk of making mistakes. The worst of all would be to do nothing in the face of the intolerable."

## References

Bakshi, Rajni. 'Beyond Market Fundamentalism'. In *The Hindu*, September 24, 2000. (New Delhi).

Dewey, John. *Democracy and Education*. New York: Free Press, 1966.

Dreze, Jean and Sen, Amartya. *India: Economic Development and Social Opportunities*. New Delhi: Oxford University Press, 1995.

Gandhi, M. K.. *Hind Swaraj*, Ahmedabad : Nav Jeevan, 1959.

Heilbroner, Robert L. *The Great Ascent*. New York : Harper A Row, 1963.

Huntington, Samuel P. *The Clash of Civilizations and the Remaking of World Order*. New Delhi: Penguin, 1997.

Kapur, Geeta. *When was Modernism*.

Myrdal, Gunnar. *Asian Drama*. London : Penguin, 1972.

Naisbitt, John and Aburdene, Patricia. *Mega Trends: 2000*. London: Pan Books, 1990.

Powys, John Cowper. *The Meaning of Culture*. Calcutta : Rupa & Co, 1960.

Rolland, Romain. *Mahatma Gandhi*. Delhi: Ministry of Publication and Broadcast, 1976.

Toffler, Alvin. *Future Shock*. New York : Bantam Books; 1970.

Whitehead, A.N. *The Aims of Education and Other Essays*. London: Ernest Benn Ltd., 1962.

# 3

# Hinduism and Its Relevance in Global Academic Scenario

Hinduism is the cradle of India. India is the land in which the roots of Hinduism are deep and firm. The moment India is detached from the soil of Hinduism it will wilt and become lifeless. It will not remain a vibrant nation. "Hinduism", says Annie Besant, "is the lifeblood of 'Bharat Mata' without which she looses its vitality and sustainability. Except Hinduism, there is no other religion whose veins are so pure and precious in which the blood of spiritual life can be made to flow. ...If Hinduism goes away from India then India will cease to exist. India will meet the fate of Egypt which has lost itself by loosing its Dharma or religion."

In Swami Vivekanand's (1982) words, Hinduism is synonymous with Dharma, and a Hindu is not a Hindu if he or she is not spiritual. He further maintains that "the Hindu religion does not consist in struggles and attempts to believe in a certain doctrine or dogma, but in realizing, not in believing, but in being and becoming. Thus the whole object of their system is by constant struggle to become perfect, to become divine to reach God, becoming perfect even as the father in heaven is perfect,' constitutes the religion of the Hindus." Having attained perfection the Hindu lives the life of bliss infinite. The ultimate of happiness being reached when it would become a universal consciousness. This miserable little prison, individuality, is forgone and the infinite 'universal individuality' is gained, "knowing which everything else become known." Hinduism is the universal and an eternal (Sanatan) religion. It has to do with all the three segments of the arrow of time: the past, the present and the future. It is a lofty, liberal, inclusive and versatile religion. Here, no insistence is laid on the only Savior, the only One Book and the only One Path. It doesn't claim or advocate that only the Hindus will be saved or emancipated and doors of salvation will remain shut for the followers of other religion and sects. Hence there has never been a religious persecution, and no one was tortured or done to death for holding a different or a new idea. 'Let hundred schools of thoughts bloom' is the ardent desire and approach of the Hindus.

Annie Besant was overwhelmed by the scientific nature of Hinduism. There is an utmost freedom of thought and inquiry and therefore numerous paths and sects found scope and space to flourish in India. Hindus believe that every religion is a process of evolving a God out of the material man, and the same God inspires us all. "To the Hindu", says Swami Vivekanand, "every man is not traveling from error to truth, but from truth to truth, from lower truth to higher truth..... and every soul is a young eagle soaring higher and higher, gathering more and more strength, till it reaches the glorious sun. The Hindus were bold thinkers in all their ideas, so bold that one spark of their thought was enough to frighten the so called bold thinkers of the West." "These brave people followed reason wherever it led to them", said Mueller, "no matter at what cost, never caring if all their best superstitions were smashed to pieces, never caring what society would think about them, or talk about them; but what they thought was right and true."

It has been taught to Hindus by the great sages that bring out through your own exertion what you have, but do not imitate, yet take what is good from other. We have many things to learn from others, that man who refuses to learn is already dead (आनो भद्रा: कतवो यंतु विश्वत:). "Learn supreme knowledge", declares Manu, "even from the man of low birth" (अन्यादपि परमधर्मम्).

Citing from the *Ishopnishad*, Will Durant (1935) says that "Into the darkness pass they who worship ignorance; into still greater darkness they who are content with knowledge. Hindu philosophy begins where European philosophy ends with an enquiry into the nature of knowledge and the limitations of reasons, it starts not with the physics of Thales and Democritus, but with the epistemology of Locke and Kant; it takes mind as that which is most immediately known, and therefore refuses to resolve it into a matter known only through mind."

## Hindutva - A Political Variant of Hinduism ?

It is surmised that the concept of "Hindutva evolved slowly during the colonial period. The seeds of which were sown in the politics of the likes of Tilak. The modern postulation of a distinct Hindu Community dates back to the second half of the nineteenth century. 'Hindutva' as a quality or property of this community was a nationalistic reconstruction of the dynamics of Indian tradition, as a linear, evolutionary, inclusive homogenization. In the case of the proponents of Hindu identity, the Brahmanical version of Indian tradition became a core, along with paternalistic (tolerant) inclusion of other groups adhering to all the other 'indigenous' schools of thought. Those included were the Buddhists, the Jains and the Sikhs (Lele, 1996).

In the perception of the leftist and the depressed class intellectuals, the idea of "Hindutva" is different from "Hinduism" in its purpose and appeal. In contrast to the religious word "Hinduism", 'Hindutva' is seen as a political project. It is also an educational project, in the sense that it seeks to create an understanding about itself and the surrounding world on the basis of a body of information and interpretation. It is also a mobilization project because it aims at generating electoral and agitational 'mass action' for the outcomes that are anticipated and desired by a conscious, manipulating elite. Unfortunately Hinduism or Hindutva, being a religion of the majority, is many a time unnecessarily and deliberately criticized to keep it at low ebb. Fanaticism, extremism and militancy of the followers of Islam being a minority religion, are rarely objected and objectively examined. Whenever the Hindus take a stand against the communalism and conversion tactics of the followers of the Semitic religions, and become a little assertive; the leftists, secularists and the champions of minority quickly get combined against Hindus to defame and malign Hinduism. All adversaries of the Hindu phenomenon want Hindus to be dull, timid and withdrawn to expand their respective religious and political domination.

In the modem days diffusion and dominance of political activity is so much wide and deep that no religion can remain unbitten by the political bug. What is the harm then if "Hindutva"-a new variant of Hinduism has some political content in its curriculum? There is no point in getting alarmed at the initiatives and steps taken to coordinate and to reach understanding between various branches of the Banyan tree of Hinduism. It is absurd to look at such attempts as a project of homogenization. On account of its inherent attributes of openness and diversity it cannot take the form of a monolith religion. At the same time its unity will be as much important and essential as its diversity. For its own sustainability Hindutva will continue to be a 'salad bowl' and not a 'melting pot'.

**Hindu Attitude to Knowledge**

In the Hindu tradition and culture, knowledge is considered sacred and highly respected. Nothing purifies as much as knowledge (नहि ज्ञानेन सहशं पवित्रमिह विघते). The children are taught in the family to be reverent to knowledge and not to spoil its sanctity by abusing it or making its wrongful application. Since knowledge has the power to liberate people from want, ignorance and degeneration it is equated with "Moksha", the fourth Purasharth. Youth is also made aware of social consequences of knowledge. Research and innovations, therefore, must be weighed against the criteria of social consequences. Ignorance governed by values is more beneficial for the society than knowledge unguided by values. Right education is an integration of knowledge with values. Gaining knowledge of physical world is not the ultimate goal of Hindus. They aspire and strive to attain spiritual or supreme knowledge, which is the knowledge of all knowledges. In-fact, knowledge is a means of acquiring humility, competence, wealth and happiness. The source of this happiness is not the fragments or small little things of this world, but the 'Bhuma' or the whole and the perfect (यो वे भूमा : तत् सुखं अल्पे न सुखं अस्ति ). Nothing can be more relevant today in this knowledge driven world than this Hindu attitude to knowledge. Impressive presence and performance of Indians (mostly Hindus) in the Silicon Valley amply demonstrate that the Hindu way of life and family ties are tremendously helpful in realizing the wealth creating potential of knowledge (Naroola, 2001).

Science denotes knowledge from observation of the outside world and conscience is the knowledge we carry within us. Science and conscience are inseparable according to the Hindu thinking. Knowledge must bring responsibility but scientists are in general, seen insufficiently aware of their wider social obligation in spite of knowing that use and abuse of science may put the very existence of human species in danger. Sir Michael Atiyah, the president of Pugwash has rightly said in his Schrodinger Lecture: "if you create something, you should be concerned with the consequences. This should apply as much to making scientific discoveries as it does to having children."

Similarly, John Polanyi (2001), Nobel Prize winner for chemistry (1986), believes that commitment to truth is also a commitment to human rights. One thing, which distinguishes the community of scientists, is the fact that it is international. But what makes it function as a community is its ethics. It has a shared ideal, which is to put the truth ahead of personal advantage. No doubt this is the age of information and ideas. But ideas deficient of wisdom and value - orientation can convert a man into a "human bomb'. Let ideas cut ideas, but not the man, the mine of ideas. In these times of 'knowledge-explosion' the rate of mortality of ideas is increasing. Hence, the pace of production of new ideas and their application must be hastened. To prevent paralysis of both the will and the ideas, we must think and act briskly, innovatively and vigorously to find out solutions of the impending problems of the nation (Chaudhari et al., 2001).

## Hindutva and Hindu Intellectuals

By and large, the so called intellegentia of India is in the grip of a complex which has made them think and feel that they can not be acknowledged as 'progressive' unless they display through their speech and writings that they are leftist and secularist in their orientation. This fear of losing their 'secu-*left*' credentials do not allow them to be footloose or objective intellectuals. Even some of them sometimes hesitate to identify themselves as Hindus, and at times the use of word Hindu is repulsive for them. An anecdote narrated by B. B. Kumar (2001), editor of *Dialogue* quarterly, in the Oct-Dec 2001 issue, throws ample light on prejudiced and subjective way of thinking of highly placed and highly educated Hindu intellectuals. An eminent Professor of Economics and Economic Advisor to the then Prime Minister Nehru, Dr. Gyanchand during his stay at Kohima made an enquiry from Dr. Kumar about the religion of Nagas. Mr. Kumar answered the question by saying that Non-Christian Nagas call themselves Hindu. Dr. Gyanchand angrily reacted and said: "no you are a fanatic". Coincidently, soon after this verbal exchange, an Angami Naga, who was a school teacher, came there. Seeing a tuff of hair on his head Mr. Kumar asked him "Are you a Christian?" quick came the reply: "No I am a Hindu". This was enough to convince Dr. Gyanchand that he was not correct in his generalization that all Nagas are Christians. But all are not amenable to facts and truths like Dr. Gyanchand.

This type of conditioning or inferiority complex owes its origin to the pro-left and secularist or minority oriented policy of Nehruvian era. Because Nehru ruled the country for a long time and enjoyed an unquestioning authority and acceptance by the people due to his participation in the struggle for independence, his views and statements were taken as pious and potable without any objective examination. With the passage of time these two tenets of his skewed policy got stabilized as the political culture of the country. His abnormal tilt towards science and secularism did a great disservice to the centuries old faith-oriented and God fearing tradition of India. Nehruvian approach to polity and society contributed a lot towards making Indians Godless and Valueless. "To say that India has a secular character," says V. S. Naipaul (1999), "is being historically unsound. Dangerous or not, Hindu militancy is a corrective to the history I have been talking about. It is a creative force and will be so. Islam can not reconcile with it."

These wrongs of Nehru's rule should be righted, and the age old long - cherished balance between material and spiritual, science and religion and technology and culture, propounded by Hinduism, be restored and reinforced. Such an attempt will enable men and women to evolve their divine nature by assimilating the transcendental or divine qualities described in the sixteenth chapter of the *Gita*. Thus they would be rearmed with morality and human values to fight against the demonic and degenerating forces of violence, exploitation, disintegration, discrimination, corruption and consumerism. In fact it is an important tenet of Hinduism that "the sheer ignorance of our own divinity makes us weak, cruel, unfriendly and prone to every kind of sin. Nothing can make us so as long as we are conscious of the divine within us."

In this context, I wish to share with you the views of Sita Ram Goyal (1994) expressed in his book: *Defence of Hindu Society*. He emphatically asserts that "Hindu society has to observe while preparing for its defence is that it should stop processing and evaluating its own heritage in terms of ideas and ideals projected by closed and pretentious ideologies." I would like to replace the word 'society' by 'intellectuals', because it is the responsibility of Hindu intellectuals to examine and evaluate their heritage in terms of its own categories of thought, and find out the real worth of Christian, Islamic, communist and modernist claims.

"The first need of the hour", says Goel (1994), "therefore, is for Hindus (intellectual) to become aware of the fundamentals of their own faith (Hindu Spirituality), the premises on which their own society has evolved (Hindu Sociology), and the vicissitudes which their own society has experienced in the march of time (Hindu History)". He further affirms that Hindus have become devoid of confidence simply because they have ceased to take legitimate, well-informed and conscious pride in their spiritual, cultural and social heritage. Here I would like to say that the 'self-concept' of Hindus has become too low and pale and their 'locus of control' has grown too much external. The sworn adversaries and competitors of Hinduism are taking advantage of the enervation of its followers, particularly the Hindu intelligentia. In view of an all round attack on Hindutva, the Hindu elites need to straighten their backbone to keep arise, awake and to stop not till the lost glory is regained.

## Simple Living : A Key to Sustainability

The current form of globalization aims at ruthless commercialization of almost everything including that of the life-sustaining gift of the nature like air and water. In the words of Karl Polanyi "capitalism has succeeded in making the bounty of nature and people's work energy into commodities. The art of healing has become a commercial industry, education a matter of degrees that can be bought". This variety of globalization evades a sharing of resources and demands conformism to western worldview. It has taken the form of market fundamentalism. Like Social Darwinism it tends to disregard altruism and cooperation. It does not reflect social and moral values, which are so essential to a civilized society. This amoral dimension of globalization can be salvaged by humanizing the market forces and by embedding economy in social relation through all embracing and life enhancing elements of Hinduism, which enable an individual to discern "all creatures in his self and his self in all creatures."

The global academic scenario is seized with the perplexing paradoxes of having poverty in plenty and helplessness amidst plethora of sophisticated weapons. We have built guided missiles but the man still remains unguided. Men and women are experiencing loneliness in the crowd. On the one hand we have ample of knowledge at our disposal but on the other we have not been able to solve the basic problems of human life. Human history is becoming more and more a race between the greed and the need of the people. The lust for consumption is overstepping the carrying capacity of the earth and the intergenerational equity is being threatened by depletion of resources. This is resulting in destitution, desperation and degeneration of the larger humanity. How far can we sustain our lives and economies by playing the 'marketing game' of creating demands by changing labels and brands or by making the products obsolete?

In this frightening situation of 'man playing wolf to man' the tried and tested philosophy and the practices of Hinduism seem relevant and defy emulation. It is well known that as ordained in the *Gita* and the *Ishavasya Upanishad*, Hindus attach a great importance to the values of sacrifice and detachment.

Simple living and high thinking has been the guiding principle of their conduct and every day living. In fact parsimonious use of materials and austere living, being an antidote to consumerism, are a key to sustainability and quality of life. Swami Vivekananda, around hundred years ago, predicted the crisis of our age and said: "In the West they are trying to solve the problem how much a man can possess, and we are trying here to solve the problem on how little a man can live on. This struggle and this difference will still go on for some centuries. But if history has any truth in it, and if prognostications ever prove true, it must be that those who train themselves to live on the least and control themselves well, will in the end win the battle, and that those who run after enjoyment and luxury, however vigorous they may seem for the moment will have to die and become annihilated" (In Akhilanand, 1965). Similar views have been expressed by Oswald Spengler in his famous work: *Decline of the West* in the early 20th century.

Besides emphasizing universal brotherhood, Hindutva or Hinduism insists on cooperative, non-exploitative and mutually nurturing relationship with nature, animal world and inanimate objects. All ancient Hindu prayers aim at the welfare, peace and prosperity of all irrespective of race, religion and nation. An enormous feeling of respect for every object and particle of the earth is cultivated and transmitted from generation to generation. This attitude is condensed in one of the verses of the Rigveda in which it is underlined that the earth is the mother and we are her sons and daughters: "भूमि : माता पुत्रोहं पृथिव्याः" It is perhaps this Vedic idea of motherhood of the earth that inspired the environmentalists and the ecologists to mobilize the world opinion and thinking to celebrate the 'Earth Day' on an international scale.

**Hindutva and Human Fraternity and Dignity**

Hinduism is basically a humanitarian religion. A special emphasis is put in the religious discourses and ideational dialogues to inculcate a liberal and all embracing outlook in the children and the youth. In the basic social institutions like family and schools, large-heartedness is fostered and small mindedness is discouraged. This is summed up in the aphorism: "अयं निजः परोवेति गणना लघुचेतसां। उदार चरितानाम् तु वसुधेव कुटुंबकं". In the scriptures it has also been stated that it is here in India that the whole world is transformed into a human nest: "यत्र भवति विश्व एक नीड़म" Renowned indologist Basham (1954) maintained that "...overall impression is that in no other part of the ancient world were the relations of man and man, and man and state, so fair and human. In no other ancient law book are their rights so well protected as in Arthashastra. No other ancient law giver proclaimed such noble ideals of fair play in battle as did Manu... to us most striking feature of ancient Indian civilization is humanity."

Another eminent scholar and historian Arnold Toynbee also took an appreciative note of the all embracing humanism pervading Hindu ethos and Indian culture and observed that "at this supremely dangerous moment in human history, the only way of salvation for mankind is the Indian way. Here we have the attitude and the spirit that can make it possible for human race to grow together into a single family and in this atomic age this is the only alternative to destroying ourselves." Thus the great and leading thinkers of the world find the ancient Hindu ways of thought and conduct very much relevant and valuable even for the modern world, because 'common humanity' is more important than our differences. Bill Clinton (2002) has rightly named the struggle for interdependence as "the struggle of the soul of the 21st century".

**Lessons from Historv and Challenge of Third Millennium**

To make Hindutva or Hinduism still more relevant for the third millennium, we the followers of Hinduism must try to discover and identify the causes which led to our defeat and set-backs in the past. We also need to liberate us from deep-seated sense of submissiveness, dependence proneness and 'Chalta Hai' mentality. We ought to confront the historical fact that "for about a thousand years, roughly between 600 B.C. and 500 A.D. India was a dynamic, progressive and prosperous nation but since slid eyeless in the Dark Ages. The state of Indian Culture at the end of the first Millennium was dismal. "... During virtually the entire dynamic phase of our civilization the religion of the dominant classes in India was Buddhism, not Hinduism. The two religions, though offshoots of the Vedic religion were entirely unlike each other. Buddhism was a demanding religion, which imposed absolute *dharmic* imperatives on human conduct and insisted that men should strive to transcend his environment and his own innate nature. In contrast Hinduism was an undemanding, I am OK you're OK religion, which accepted ethical pluralism, assigned to each caste its own dharma and advised men to be contented with his lot, however despicable his lot might be. Buddhism inculcated discipline and endeavour, Hinduism inculcated passivity and fatalism. The emphasis of Buddhism was on conduct, that of Hinduism on faith (Eraly, 1999)." No doubt the latter's soft and undemanding version of Hinduism has done much harm to the Hindu society. Let us revert back to the original *"Tap Sah Vijayam"* 'hard work brings victory' form of Hinduism.

Secondly, all forms of discrimination, segregation and disparities should be eliminated to make social justice as the main stay of the Hindu society. The weak should be made strong and the strong just to revive the dignity of man and the dignity of labour in the society. The 'worth' of the individual and not the 'birth' be the sole criterion of men and women's vertical mobility. Thirdly we are required to get ourselves set and equipped to meet the demand of 21st Century in terms of quality, creativity, morality and professionalism. We have survived many onslaughts in our history, but to survive in rapid pace of change and competitive climate of the third millennium we need an all together different strategy of making swift but steady preparation and of compressing time to deliver goods not just in time but before the deadline. Certainly, to make this happen initiative, innovativeness and enterprising spirit are needed on the part of those who take pride in calling themselves Hindus.

We are living in a Knowledge Worker Age. Unlike the earlier 'control and obedience centered' Industrial Age, this new age demands openness and participation in the institutions and organizations. It needs new or different set of knowledge, skill and attitude. In this age, leadership is distributive and it communicates to the people their worth and potential so clearly that they come to see it in themselves. People or workers are enabled and empowered to have self-control, in a high trust environment so that they feel free to tap into their talents.

The great scholar of civilization Arnold Toynbee has said, in an unconventional way, that: "nothing fails like success". In the times of rapid social change it is true, because when your response is equal to a challenge, you are successful. But when you face new challenge, the old response fails to work. Perhaps, that is why, it is called a failure. Hence, in the days of change when complexity and uncertainly are increasing we are under a cognitive constraint to discover a new response to a new challenge. This is a challenge of change for the followers of all religions to remain relevant in the global academic scenario.

## References

Akhilanand, Swami (1965). *Hindu Psychology : Its Meaning for the West.* Longon : Routledge & Kegal Paul Ltd. Ch XIV. p. 215.

Basham, A.L. (1954). *The Wonder that was India.* New Delhi: Rupa & Co.

Chaudhari U.S. et al. (2001) 'Sustainable Socio-Economic Reforms in the Information Age: Initiatives and Imperatives.' In M.L. Sodhi (ed), *Towards a New Era: Economic Social and Political Reforms.* New Delhi: Har - Anand Publications.

Clinton, Bill (2002), 'World without Walls: Struggle for this Century's Soul.' *The Times of India.* January 11, 2001.

Eraly, Abraham (1999). "1000 Years Ago: India in the 11th Century : A Mixture of Pearls and Dung" *Outlook.* November 15, 1999.

Goel, Sita Ram (1994). *Defence of Hindu Society.* New Delhi: Voice of India.

Kumar, B.B. 'Editorial Perspective'. *Dialogue* (Quarterly) (Delhi: Astha Bharti), 3(2), Oct-Dec 2001.

Lele, Jayant (1996) 'Hindutva as Pedagogic Violence' In Migel Crook (ed.). *The Transmission of Knowledge in South Asia.* Delhi: Oxford University Press.

Naipaul, V. S. (1999). Interviews taken by Tarun J. Tejpal. In *Outlook.* November 15, 1999.

Naroola, Gurmeet (2001). *The Entrepreneurial Connection: East Meets West in the Silicon.*

*Valley.* New Delhi: Tata McGraw - Hill Publishing Company Ltd.

Vivekanand, Swami (1982). *Hinduism.* Mylapore, Madras: Shri Ram Krishna Math.

# 4

# Attaining Three Goals of Higher Education

We are living in a fast changing world, and a relatively less stable society. The world is being globalized, and the developing countries are experiencing the impact of the globalizing process on their systems of education. Since the modern society and economy are increasingly becoming knowledge and idea based, higher education, being a knowledge enterprise, is expected to play an unprecedented role to face the challenges of unfolding twenty first century and the third millenium. Higher education is a modernizing influence and it is, by and by, becoming a condition for survival, as demands for advance knowledge, innovative ideas and higher skills get increased in the present competitive global environment.

## Idea and Purpose of a University

During the school period the student has been mentally bending over his desk. At the university he should stand up, look around and raise his hand to ask questions to satisfy his epistemic curiosity and to register his protest against domesticating and obscurantist forces and ideas. The spirit of generalization of ideas dominate a university. The stage of generalization is the period of entrance into manhood, therefore the students are enabled to proceed from the particular towards the general ideas, and study their applications to concrete cases. A well-planned university course is therefore, expected to be a study of 'the wide sweep of generality'.

"The justification for a university", says A.N. Whitehead (1962), "is that it preserves the connection between knowledge and zest for life, by uniting the young and the old in the imaginative consideration of learning. The university imparts information, but imparts imaginatively...............Imagination is not to be divorced from the facts. It is a way of illuminating the facts..............The task of a university is to weld together imagination and experience..............A university is imagination or it is nothing - at least nothing useful".

It is fascinating to recall that two great thinkers—Jawaharlal Nehru and Cardinal Newman, though coming from different countries, thought of the idea of university in the same year, that is, 1947. In Nehru's perception "an university stands for humanism, for tolerance, for reason, for the adventure of ideas and for the search of truth. It stands for the onward march of the human race towards even higher objectives". On the other hand Cardinal Newman underscores training as an aim of university education. He says that a training is, the great ordinary means to a great but ordinary end. In his estimate "a university aims at raising the intellectual tone of society; at cultivating the public mind; at purifying the material taste; at supplying true principles to popular enthusiasm and fixed aims to popular aspiration; at giving enlargement and soberiety to the ideas of the age; at facilitating the exercise of political power, and refining the intercourse of private life." Infact, these are broad societal goals of higher education and not classroom confined objectives of teaching.

The territory of higher education is generally addressed as 'kingdom of mind', as if it has not much to do with the 'life of the heart'. Lord Curzon, in his convocation address to Calcutta university in 1903 took care of this aspect and described "university as a human smithy where character is forged in the furnace of experience and beaten on the anvil of truth". In his earlier convocation address of 1900, he expressed an utter dissatisfaction with the performance of Indian universities. He said: "Indian Universities inculcate a hybrid morality and nourish a 'bastard civilization'." While exploring the human nature of a university, Robert Goheen (1969) asked an interesting and significant question: "Where in your society can a person disagree with impunity from accepted practices, dogmas and doctrines?" He himself gave the answer: "In the universities". This enlightening answer reaffirms the role of universities as abodes of 'dissenting conscience' of the society, and not an assembly of anti-intellectual psychophants and satellites. But, surely, this function begs the presence of scholars of high moral conduct, integrity and courage, for "great universities and timid people go ill-together." The academic entrepreneurs engaged in the pursuit of excellence and creativity, know no confines, limits and boundaries, and choose the 'road less travelled by'.

The loci of higher education, such as universities play central role in the production of concepts, ideologies, and ways of thinking as well as their production, through curricula, graduate lectures, post graduate seminars, the supervision of doctoral thesis and research projects and in the organization of workshops and conferences. Universities prepare the generation that will run the state, the institutions of civil society and economic enterprises. They also participate in the moulding of intellectual environment of the future (both medium and long term). In the present social situation, the colleges and universities are expected to prepare and produce such enterprizing young people "Who are easy to lead, but difficult to drive, who are easy to govern but impossible to enslave." Even Swami Vivekanand was in vigorous search of a band of such 'Nachiketas', 'Prahalads' and 'Abhimanyus' who could behave and make a difference to the existing sociopolitical muddle and miasma. Infact, these are the people who should have a thinking head own their shoulders, and they should call, their minds their own without agitating their bodies. 'Robots' and 'clones' type of young people being grromed by the universities can not initiate a change, because robots can not rebel and clones do not have the originality.

The universities should be viewed as the institutional locus par excellence by which, on the one hand, intellectual resistance can be organized to the totalitarian tendencies of racism, sexism and belligerence; and on the other, an intervention to regulate the rapid and rampant change. Change is life itself. But, unguided and unrestrained change overwhelms not only man's physical defences but his decisional processes as well. To Toffler (1970), such a change is the enemy of life. This is a type of cancer in history which may give birth to deadly diseases like war, ecological degradation, racism, obscene contrast between rich and poor, the revolt of the young, and the rise of mass irrationalism. "A future-facing higher education system can help create the consciousness needed for man to undertake the control of change and the guidance of his revolution. For, by making imaginative use of change to channel change, we can spare ourselves the trauma of future shock, and can reach out to humanize distant tomorrows (Toffler, 1970)".

In the foregoing analysis and discussion, so far, I have identified and enumerated the aims and functions of higher education. Now, an attempt will be made to show as to how teaching, research and extension work can be directed to accomplish and serve those purposes.

### Teaching

Creation, preservation, transmission and application of knowledge, upgrading of skills and refining the taste and attitudes are considered the basic functions of higher education. Research creates knowledge and also assess what knowledge is worthy of preservation and application. Through the act of teaching, knowledge or cultural heritage is transmitted to those who enter into the institutions of higher learning for higher studies. Infact, teaching is not simply a matter of dissemination of knowledge but of scholarship, transforming and extending knowledge by a process of classroom debate and a continual examination and challenging of both content and methodology.

Knowledge now doubles every five years and its 'shelf life' (as evidenced from the US citation index) is falling fast, from eight years in 1975 to four years in 2000. Half of what a person learns is no longer valid when he or she reaches middle age. In future, facts will falter and information will wear out, and ideas and skills will obsolesce at a more rapid rate. Therefore, in order to arrest professional obsolescence, people of all professions must learn continuously and develope a 'knack of learning'. The professors of a modern university or college ought to regard themselves primarily as learners, and as teachers only secondarily. Pedagogical preparation is equally necessary to turn professors into teachers, who can facilitate classroom transactions. Professors are expected to be people put on perfection - bubbling with excitement over ideas. They should read, write and speak great thoughts. Z.F. Bereday asks them to 'hitch their wagon to the highest stars'.(Chaudhari, 1986).

Teachers have reduced the classrooms to lesson hearing rooms. Teaching has degenerated into an anti-dialogical activity, in which students are told about the facts, concepts, principles and theories and they commit them to memory as passive learners. Students are rarely stimulated to put questions and actively participate in the process of teaching and learning. Really speaking, a classroom is an encouraging and inspiring place where teachers, under their intellectual influence, initiate and engage the students in the process of inquiry and discovery to ultimately make them active investigators, autonomous learners and independent thinkers.

The scholarship of teaching is in the process of transformation by new and increasingly complex technology. Some of the routine activities of the teachers will be taken-up by the technotronic devices, but the breath of life has to be communicated by the teacher through the dramatic influence of his or her personality. The subject of educational technology has come to stay, and its role in enhancing learning effectiveness has been recognized. In higher education teachers should not hesitate to employ technology as their assistant, since educational technology can help them with special reference to the design and content of instructional materials, their delivery, assessment and feedback. With increase in the use of technology in teaching and learning, the role of the teacher will be expected to be quite different from what it was in traditional classroom teaching. In the technology-mediated or assisted learning and teaching, the teacher is the author, playwright, actor, director and mentor, with actor's role assuming the major significance. New technology will afford more opportunity to the learner for individualized and self-paced learning. Application of technology in the classroom and in other non-formal settings, will make available more free time to the teachers, which could be profitably employed for better planning, innovative practices and production of creativity inducing instructional material (Natrajan, 1999).

Parker J. Palmer (1997) in her book: *The courage to Teach*, says that "the courage to teach is the courage to keep one's heart open in those very moments when the heart is asked to hold more than it is able, so that teacher and students and subject can be woven into the fabric of community that learning and living require". She also pleads that good teaching needs 'exploration of the inner landscape' of a teacher's life, and inter weaving of intellect, emotion and spirit. Teaching, like any truly human activity, emerges from one's inwardness, for better or worse. In a very personal and persuasive tone, the author further pours her heart into the words and says that "as I teach, I project the condition of my soul on to my students, my subject and our ways of being together. The entanglements I experience in the classroom are often no more or less than the convolutions of my inner life. Viewed from this angle, teaching holds a mirror to the soul. If I am willing to look in that mirror, and not run away from what I see, I have a chance to gain self-knowledge, and knowing myself is as crucial to good teaching as knowing my students and my subject". 'This approach: "courage to teach", suggested and advocated by Palmer, would no doubt go a long way in shaping the character and personality of the students besides initiating the process of learning how to learn'.

**Research**

"Education is discipline for the adventure of life; research is intellectual adventure", says A.N. Whitehead (1962), and "the universities should be "homes of adventure' shared in common by young and old. For successful education there must always be a certain freshness in the knowledge dealt with. It must either be new in itself or it must be invested with some novelty of application to the new world of new times. " Whitehead is also of the opinion that a progressive society depends upon its inclusion of three groups - scholars, discoverers and inventors. Its progress also depends upon the fact that its educated masses are composed of members each with a tinge of scholarship, a tinge of discovery, and a tinge of invention. Universities are the chief agencies for this fusion of progressive activities into an effective instrument of progress. In the area of research and discovery now the universities are not unique or monopoly institutions. The research and knowledge production function has been shouldered by number of other institutions like non-university institutes, research centres, government agencies, industrial laboratories, think tanks and consultancies. The scholarship of application is transformed by this social distribution of the creation of knowledge which must now be "carried out in a context of application.......socially accountable and reflexive." (Gilbbons, M. et. al., 1994).

Research and teaching are not competitive but mostly complementary and cooperative partners. One may suffer on account of apathy of the other. Research findings update teaching and teaching encounters make available subject-matter and problems for investigation to the researcher. Unfortunately, a chasm between research and teaching has been created since the day the research activity acquired glamour and snob-value. A teacher who teaches for name-sake, and possesses the ability to create lot of fuss about research is generally regarded as a smart and superior teacher. In initial selections for entry into teaching profession, and later on for promotions, research is given more attention and weightage than sincere and effective teaching. As a consequence of this trend, 'publish or perish' syndrome gained greater importance than 'teach or terminate' and 'serve or severe' phenomenon.

It is said that if you want your teachers to be imaginative, ask them to do research. No doubt, research keeps a teacher intellectually trim, and it acts as an antidote to intellectual death. It refreshes both the researcher-teacher and the teacher-researcher. Therefore, teachers must engage themselves in research. But, again, emphasis could be mis-placed if teachers run after the latest fashion and frills for doing research, instead of what is genuinely required to be researched to tackle the day-to-day problems or to examine the fundamentals of teaching and learning in view of the changing national and international scenario.

Research is learnt by doing and taught by contagion. Therefore, while providing training in research at Master's and M.Phil. levels, students should systematically and seriously be initiated in the activity of research. Here, the supervisors have to play a mentor's role. Being a materially poor country India can not afford a 'messing together' or 'rehashing rigmarole' in research. It is estimated that around 25% researches in science and 40% in social sciences and humanities are substandard. The quality of researches done at Masters' level is very poor. Many a Ph.D. theses are stuffed with blown up bibliographies and plethora of footnotes to gloss over the deficiency of the research report. Perhaps, because of this tendency of the researchers, a Ph.D. thesis is compared with the face of an ugly rich lady who spends lot of money to hide her uglyness with the help of cosmetics and ornaments.

Research, completed for Master and Ph.D. degrees, is expected to make atleat some difference to the existing situation, if it does not make any original contribution. It should also give an evidence of understanding the science involved in the process of research and in the presentation of the report. The intellectual height of higher education must get reflected genuinely in all those products which are an outcome of teaching and research. Replacing the word 'philosophy' by 'research', I would like to reproduce below a very important statement made by John W. Gardner (1962) in his well known book: *Excellence.* "The society which scorns excellence in plumbing because plumbing is a humble activity and tolerates shoddiness in 'research' because it is an exalted activity, will have neither good plumbing nor good 'research'. Neither its pipes nor its theories will hold water"

**Extension or the Third Dimension**

Higher education is pre-eminently social thing in its origin and function. Since it is created by the society, it is primarily required to serve the society by making available suitable personnel, goods and services for meeting various needs of the society. Owing to the elitist character of the universities, teaching and research got precedence over the most important function of serving the masses who are socio-economically and culturally deprived. Though the University Education commission (1948-49) invited the attention of the University Community and the government towards their indifference to rural India and disadvantaged section, yet no awakening towards this function was visible for a long time. Even the recommendations for establishing 'Rural Universities' and 'Janta Colleges' were not taken enthusiastically and seriously. The Education Commission (1964-66) also pleaded for incorporation of socially relevant contents in the programmes of the universities" and also for bridging the gap between gown and town, that is university and the community in the neighbourhood. The first phase of activities in the area of extension services started when the policy frame of UGC in 1977 insisted on giving equal importance to extension as a 'Third dimension' in addition to Teaching and Research, if the university system has to discharge adequately its responsibilities to the entire education system and to the society as a whole. Further impetus was given to the 'Third dimension' or extension by the National Policy of Education (1986).

Ramlal Parikh Committee recommended that "the university system should absorb the concept of 'extension culture' as its integral component and a beginning be made by providing at least 25% time allocation for the off-campus extension work through community education type of programrre". Infact, through organization of regular and systematic extension programmes, the illiterate, dehumanized and deprived people can be conscientized or awakened to help themselves. By participating in extension work, the students and teachers get opportunities to enrich their own experience, come to know the social reality and get sensitized to abject poverty, illiteracy and destitution. A unity of outlook and faith between the masses and the intelligentia is also achieved. University and college people also get an opportunity to apply their knowledge and expertise in enabling disadvantaged masses to identify, analyse and solve their problems.

Extension services aims at developing confidence, and raising self-concept of the depressed people so that they can become their own leaders and change-agents. University Community can also make available the results of their research and deliberations to NGOs, industrial groups, and govt. agencies which work for the upliftment and empowerment of weaker section of the society. Thus, a variety of non-formal ways and programmes can be designed to reach out to the needy and down-trodden to equip them to 'celebrate awareness' and to agitate to get suitable opportunity and space in the polity and society.

Extension work is a cultural action for freedom and dignity for the suffering masses. In view of this assumption, the following general objectives (George *et.al.*, 1998) can be set to provide direction to the extension workers:

1. To assist people to identify their needs and problems for the purpose of analysis and solution.
2. To enable them to be their own leaders and masters by learning the art and skill to organize themselves for disciplined action.
3. To disseminate the results of their thinking and research for consumption by the people at large, in simple and comprehensible language.
4. To awaken people to mobilize and utilize resources which they have and they need from outside.
5. To collect from the field information and issues for intellectual incubation and resolution, and also to reconceptualize curricular contents and research problems in the light of this field information.
6. To ultimately, arouse a dissatisfaction and disquiet towards dehumanizing plight of the masses so that they become their own liberator.

The methodology for working with the community should involve affectionate and intimate conversation and, 'heart to heart talk' to the people. Paulo Friere has described this approach in the following beautiful words:

> "Go to the people. Live among them. Love them. Learn from them. Plan with them. Start with what they know. Build on what they have. Then the people will say : "We have done it".

In the end, I would like to draw your attention towards almost complete break-down and collapse of higher education in the country, and a widespread attitude of indifference and cynicism towards the crisis. "Cynicism of the profession', says

J.D. Sethi (1983), "is complete. Indeed, the profession constitutes a social club of those who refuse to behave as academics but nevertheless insist on being called intellectuals. The vice-chancellors, the comic figures of the contemporary educational scene also make the same claim. In this club, which is ordered to defend the status of the politicians and bureaucrats, dissent is no longer honoured. Hence no debate is possible."

Nearly 42 years ago Kothari Education Commission (1964-66) diagnosed the standards of higher education on the criteria of adequacy, dynamism and international comparability, and made the following observation :-

"Judged on the basis of these criteria, the existing situation appears to be far from satisfactory. Our universities do a good deal of work which really belongs to the secondary school and the latter in turn does a good deal of work of the primary school.......The weakness of these degrees was pointed out by the Calcutta University Commission more than forty years ago. But the situation has not materially changed to this day. Meanwhile advanced countries have made phenomenal progress in education. The gap between their standards and ours has further widened."

At this juncture, I feel that a determined intellectual minority must come forward from the teaching community to revolt against the decayed system to make an impact and undertake, in the words of J.D. Sethi, three exercises: one of exposure of the existing system, second of retaliating against it and third, of producing an alternative. All the three exercises must go together.

The twenty first century will be ruthlessly competitive. Our competitors will not behave like our brothers and sisters. If we wish the new generations to survive and succeed in the 'brave new world', we must rebuild the edifice of higher education on the magnificent and marvellous four pillars of quality, creativity, professionalism and morality. We must remember that "it is not the big that beat the small, but the fast that beat the slow".

## References

Chaudhari, U.S., *Issues and Advances in Education,* Delhi ; Ajanta International Books, 1986.

Gardner, John F. *Excellence : Can we be Equal and Excellent too?* Delhi: Universal Book Stall, 1961.

Gibbons M., et. al., *The New Production of Knowledge*. London: Sage, 1994.

Goheen, Robert, *The Human Nature of a University*, 1969.

George, S.J. and Sooryamoorthy R., *Extension in Higher Education*, Delhi: Vikas, 1998.

Natrajan, R., Science, Technology and the Challenge of the XXI Century. *University News*, 37(20), 1999.

Nehru, J.L., *Convocation Address*, Allahabad University, 1947.

Newman, J.H. Cardinal, *The Idea of a University,* New York: Longman Green and Co., 1947.

Palmer, Parker J., *The Courage to Teach : Exploring the Inner Landscape of a Teacher's Life*, San Francisco: Jossy Bass Publishers, 1997.

Report of the *Education Commission (1964-66),* Delhi: Ministry of Education, 1966.

Sethi, J.D., *The Crisis and Collapse of Higher Education in India,* Delhi: Vikas Publishing House, 1983.

Tosffler, Alvin, *Future Shock,* New York: Bantam Books, 1970.

Whitehead, A.N., *The Aims of Education and other Essays*, London: Ernest Beam Ltd., 1962.

# 5

# "Teaching-Research" Nexus and Knowledge Society

Due to our preference for 'acquisition of information', and a lack of orientation to the 'inquiry' model in education, for a long time, teaching and research remained two independent or separated territories in our country. It is around seventies, research gained momentum, after the recommendation of the **Kothari Education Commission** in 1966, that research be made a basic component of education. Infact, it took a long time for the scholars and educationists, the world over, to see the importance and utility of the connection between teaching and research. It is perhaps, in the beginning of the last decade of the 20th century, findings of researches on 'teaching-searching' nexus, prompted the academics to realize that the process of teaching will become stagnant and dull if it is not fertilized and rejuvenated by the researches. Clark (1991, 1997) insisted that the 'unity of teaching and research as advocated by Wilhem Von Humboldt in Germany, is needed to be revived. A broadening from concept of research to that of "disciplined inquiry" enabled the scope of university forms of inquiry to be widened to include applied research, research and development as well as scholarship. It is generally agreed that all university teachers should get involved in one or other form of disciplined inquiry, even if only a minority can be involved in research in the traditional meaning of the word. Obviously, within the range of 'disciplined inquiry' lies the potential for the broader critical intellectual function.

Today, we live in a 'Knowledge society', that really is an 'inquiring society'. In this changed society, the academics have highlighted "functional interdependence" of two academic roles of teaching and researching. It is embedded in a world in which academic definitions of knowledge and higher education remain largely dominant. An extension and an embedding of an inquiry-based model of education is a requisite for this type of society wherein the "research-teaching-study" nexus would be a key component. Knowledge societies depend upon continuing systematic or disciplined inquiry to drive them economically and socially, and to solve their problems. Barnett (2000) depicts a world, but he depicts and focuses strongly on its complexity. It is a world, he argues, in which there are multiple and competing frameworks for understanding and problem solving, that not only change but also are not necessarily commensurable. This implies changing concept of academic work. In their research function, academics are required to be responsible for "contributing to the super complexity of the life-world", creating new conceptual and epistemological frameworks, and also promoting public understanding of and engagement with this notion of the world. In their teaching function, they will be helping their students not only to manage, but also to prepare themselves to contribute 'new frameworks and idea-kits' through which super complexity of the world can be understood and coped with.

The knowledge society is centred on the need for students to develop critical and constructionist conception of knowledge, truth and meaning, because knowledge, truth and meaning are not given in this society. They are to be explored and constructed in interaction and collaboration with others. This approach is necessary to cope with a changing knowledge environment. Implicit herein is an academic commitment to and involvement in research as the key to designing and implementing teaching strategies through which students are enabled to understand and appreciate that knowledge is contextually defined and contested. It is constructed within epistemic communities, institutions and/or networks with their own goals, histories, pre-suppositions, epistemic rules and conceptual frameworks. Students are assisted to move from a naive stance towards existing knowledge and its creation to an informed ability to criticize, analyse and investigate it by understanding how it is developed within their own chosen discipline or subject. Thus, they are groomed and prepared for participation in the research as well as being given opportunities to demonstrate that they have grasped a range of research structures, methods and approaches (Baxter Magolda, 1999). Thus, this learner-centered investigatory approach invokes and involve the human act of making meaning and making sense of phenomena.

Maurice Kogan (2004) has tried to explicate the "potential range of inquiry" vis-a-vis the university teacher, and he has also described the characteristics necessary for research and teaching. He confirms the common observation that there is a great deal of overlap.

"Both require: mastery of substantive subject matter; an ability to conceptualize; to be conversant with main concepts and theories; the ability to present and disseminate research findings; to engage in collective administrative chores within basic unit; participation in disciplinary or subject area outside their own institution and country; ability to supervise and examine doctoral learning methods for varied groups and levels of students. There are tasks and skills that are specific to the two activities, however such as, for researcher, creating research questions or seeking research funding and, for teachers, converting research findings into curriculum or developing teaching methods. So, both combination and separation are feasible".

**Researches on 'Teaching-research' Nexus: The Student Perspective**

The research-teaching nexus is important to the identities of academics and good teachers. It is far more visible in science than in social science. Mostly, discussions in institutions of higher learning tend to be research-centred emphasizing what the teacher brings to the educational process, including how that is influenced by being a researcher. Concepts of learning and learner are far less discussed. It is very often done in the context of the relationship between teaching and learning rather than that between research and learning or the academic researcher and the student learner. Doing research necessarily makes the teachers confront with new developments in the area of theoretical concepts, methods and models. This in turn, makes them more sympathetic and understanding to students, but also more demanding of high standards of achievement.

It is contestable to say that research is the sole or even primary source of enthusiasm for the subject. But it can be said with greater confidence that research acts as an antidote to intellectual stagnation. This is supported by the scientist philosopher Polanyi (1973) who says that "passion and intellectual vibrancy are deeply welded into one another." Research into student's views of the "research-teaching nexus" is still relatively scarce but this is growing or changing. Presently, at least two sets of studies have been reported. One, by Ruth Neumann (1994) in Australian universities and the other by Alan Jenkings *et al.* at a post-1992 UK university (Brean and Lindsay, 1999; Lindsay *et al.,* 2002). Both sets of studies included undergraduate and postgraduate students. In the British study, students studying Master's courses, and in Australian study the doctoral students were included. The importance for (and of) student motivation of research-teaching relationship is a strong theme in both these research studies. These studies present substantial evidence that teacher's involvement in research can and does enhance many student's motivation to study their subject. Students made strong links between this and the enthusiasm of their teachers, which they saw as a function of their involvement in research.

Students in their comments reflect an understanding of the research-teaching link in both tangible and intangible terms. They strongly appreciated those of their teacher's lectures who passed on new knowledge from their research. Science students in the UK university saw it as essential to them that their courses introduced them to the cutting edge of their discipline. Science students in Australian universities were particularly excited when they got the opportunity, not only to learn research skills and new techniques from their teacher's own current work, but also to undertake experiments themselves. In the Australian study, it was revealed that direct exposure of contemporary research and the research process had enabled students to develop questioning and critical approaches to knowledge and to articulate a sense of knowledge as continually evolving and changing in both science and social science. It was also seen that research-teaching connection was less evident in humanities subjects than in the science and social sciences. Thus, the researches demonstrate that various aspects of the research-teaching nexus have meaning and value for the students at different levels and in variety of contexts.

Research findings also suggest that academic concepts of knowledge and higher education continue to have influence and that a range of students have benefited from being part of academic cultures, including achieving high level of epistemological sophistication. Some categories of students are articulating for themselves needs for access to research. Undergraduates were found more passive and dependent and saw it as teacher's responsibility to capture their interest and present them with current knowledge. However, the findings also suggest caution about insisting on research-led teaching for all students in higher education. Such caution might be reinforced in a mass or universal system of higher education by Neumann's (1994) findings that a further factor determining whether or not students derived benefits from a research-teaching nexus is access to close and frequent contact with their teachers. It is also not altogether clear how far research based teaching affects student motivation, as distinct from tuning into it (Henkel, 2004).

According to Henkel (2004) academics and students from a relatively wide range of institutions testify to what the 'research-teaching' nexus means for them and why they value it. Research-informed teaching and learning are seen important by them for the following considerations:

(a) the acquisition and critical appreciation of substantive knowledge in the context of assumptions that: knowledge is partial and in process of development and revision within a regulated environment;

(b) understanding of the processes through which that knowledge is acquired;

(c) learning the skills to practice 'disciplined inquiry' sanctioned by an epistemic community or institution.

## References

Barnett, R. (2000). *Realizing the University in an Age of Supercomplexity*. Buckingham and Philedalphia : SRHE and Open University Press.

Baxter Magolda (1999). *Impact of the Undergraduate Summer Scholar Experience on Epistemological Development*, Florida University of Miami.

Breen, R. and R. Lindsay (1999). "Academic Research and Student Motivation", *Studies in Higher Education*, 24(1), 75-93.

Clark, B.R. (1991), "The Fragmentation of Research, Teaching and Study: An Explorative Essay" in M.A. Trow and T. Nybom (eds.), *University and Society: Essays on the social Role of Research and Higher Education*. London: Jessica Kingsley Publishers, 101-111.

Clark, B.R. (1997), "The Modern Integration of Research activities with Teaching and Learning", *Journal of Higher Education, 68(3), 241-255.*

Henkel, Mary (2004). "Teaching and Research: The Idea of a Nexus", *Higher Education Management and Policy*, 16(2), OECD.

Jenkins, A. et al. (2003). *Reshaping Teaching in Higher Education: Linking Teaching with Research*, London: Kogan Page.

Kogan, Maurice (2004). "Teaching and Research: Some framework Issues", *Higher Education Management and Policy, 16(2)*, 9-18.

Lindsay, R.R. et al. (2002) "Academic Research and Teaching Quality: The views of Undergraduate and Post Graduate Students", *Studies in Higher Education*, 27(3).

Neumann, R. (1994). "The Teaching-Research Nexus: Applying a Framework to University Students' Learning Experiences", European Journal of Education, 29(3), 323-339.

Polanyi, M. (1973). Personal Knowledge: Towards a Post-critical Philosophy, London: Routledge and Kogan Paul.

# 6

# Ill Fated Autonomy of Universities: Diagnosis and Remedy

Modern Indian University system has no umbilical link with the indigenous ancient system of higher education. "In fact the break from the past", says Kaul (1988), "is so sudden that a visitor from the Mars would find in the modern Indian Universities a tattered version of a Scottish University rather than a chip of Taxila or Nalanda." Sir Eric Ashby (1962) has diagnosed the causes of failure of the university to meet the challenge of Indian Society. He has reached to the conclusion that the decisions made between 1835 and 1854 are undoubtedly the causes responsible for the rootlessness of the entire system of higher education of the country. The whole quantum of oriental learning and religion was excluded from university studies for half a century, and people were purveyed to a history and philosophy whose roots grounded exclusively in the mediterranean and christianity. The examinable skeleton of European civilization was communicated without ensuring that the values and standards which give flesh to these bones are also transmitted. The external paraphernalia of a university was set up without a warmth and fellowship of academic community. Infact, these are the handicaps against which Indian Universities are still struggling, and they prevent the university from becoming the centre and focus of India's intellectual life. It is perhaps, because of these handicaps, and particlarly due to lack of cohesive university community, the valuable concepts of autonomy, academic freedom and accountability could not take deeper roots in the soil of universities.

Academic freedom flourishes in an ambience of autonomy, and autonomy blossoms in the climate of accountability. Undoubtedly, these three concepts form an inevitable triangle of collective consciousness of the university community. Academic freedom is an embodiment of the 'spirit' of an organization. It is exercised by standing firmly and rationally, not in defiance but in defence, of the idea and ideal of university. Academic freedom encourages and enables a teacher to discharge his obligations of teaching, research and extension in accordance with his conscience and conviction in the wider interest of the society, without engaging in any sort of propaganda or indoctrination. Accountability, on the other hand, is an act of moral commitment to the profession, institution and society to disburse as much social return as possible. Accountability, thus, gives support and credence to the cause of autonomy.

Goheen (1969), in his book: *The Human nature of a University*, has asked a significant question: "Where in your society can a person disagree with impunity from accepted practices, dogmas and doctrines? " A very appropriate answer he has given is : "In the universities". Therefore, the universities have a major responsibility to create an intellectual climate in the country which is encouraging to the pursuit of scholarship, truth and excellence. In such a permissive climate, it is possible for the scholars to engage themselves in informed criticism, constructive disagreement and innovative practices.

Universities are required to serve as 'conscience of the society' and as 'assessors of life of the nation'. To discharge this function high standards of conduct and integrity is expected from all the members of the academic community. Besides winning public confidence, the scholars are also needed to be courageous and fearless. In the *Report of the Education Commission (1964-66)*, it has been correctly observed that "Great Universities and timid people go ill together". To achieve the objective of free inquiry, uninhabited search and adventure of ideas, universities should be treated as 'republics of professors' and 'sanctuary of scholars'? In other words, they should be granted autonomy in conducting the affairs of teaching, research, extension and expression of opinions without fear or favour.

Autonomy is the ability to make your own decisions about what to do rather than being influenced by someone else or told what to do. These days universities are established by an Act or Legislation. This legal instrument determines the scope of academic activities and executive powers of the university. Hence a university remains autonomous to the extent it adheres to the provisions of the Act and the statues. There are some draconian and abominable provisions, in the Acts of state universities, which on promulgation by the state govt. render the office of the vice-chancellor automatically vacant. Provisions of some clause of the statutes prevents a university teacher even from writing a letter to the editor of a newspaper. In the university Acts of many states provision of 'pleasure clause' has been made. This means that a Vice-Chancellor's stay in office is dependent on the pleasure of the Chancellor. In some states attempts have been made by the government to take away the powers of the Chancellor to appoint the Vice-Chancellors.

According to the *Report of the Committee on the Governance of Universities and Colleges (1971)*, "autonomy is a condition precedent if the universities are to discharge their duties and obligations effectively and efficiently as regards imparting and advancement of knowledge and also making their unique contribution to the life and development of the nation." It is further stated in the report that autonomous governance is per se a superior and more virtuous form of governance for the universities.

Consensus does not emerge among university teachers on 'why', 'how' and 'how much' autonomy is to be given to the universities. Some recommend unfettered and full autonomy to the universities, others favour granting it in measured quantity, and still others wish to withold it completely until the universities deserved this privilege. Different opinions are also expressed about administrative, academic and financial autonomy. In the present times of 'resource crunch' the question of financial autonomy has gained paramount importance. Reduction or withdrawal of financial assistance by the government and the grant-in-aid agencies would not only emaciate the autonomy but adversely affect the educational interests of weaker section of society who deserve protection from the welfare states.

There is nothing sacrosanct about the idea of autonomy. Autonomy is not absolute. It can not eradicate all the ills of universities. It is simply a means or model of governance to attain the objectives of experimentation, and to insulate universities from external pressures, influences and interference. Autonomy is an opportunity and a challenge to the universities to master and model the idea and spirit of democracy in the administrative as well as the academic activities so that the "'weak members of the university community can be made strong, and strong just'. Autonomy is not a 'touch me not' approach but it is always open to correction and guidance from outside. There are three, somewhat overlapping levels at which autonomy of universities has to function* :

---

* Report of Education Commission (1964-66).

1. *Autonomy within a university*: This means autonomy of the teaching departments or school of studies, colleges, teachers and students in relation to the university as a whole.
2. Autonomy of a university in relation to the university system, that is, the autonomy of one university in relation to another and /or in relation to the UGC and in IUB, and
3. Autonomy of the university system as a whole, including the UGC and the IUB, in relation to agencies and influences emanating from outside that system. The most important of which are the central and the State Governments.

To strike a balance in exercising autonomy of the universities, the following freedoms are granted to them:

1. Admission and examination of students,
2. Appointment of staff and removal,
3. The curricula and standard of courses,
4. The balance between teaching and research,
5. Freedom to choose direction of development keeping in view the local, national and global imperatives and trends.

There is a section of academic community in the country and outside which think that the dream of autonomy can be realized only in such universities and institutes, which are 'large enough to matter and small enought to care'. They also believe that institutions of higher education can be governed effeciently even without the formal sanction of autonomy. Ultimately, autonomy depends on the attitude and outlook of the people who operate it, since 'autonomy' begins and ends in the minds of men. Younger and junior teachers have expressed their fear that in small units or school of studies, under the control of autocratic heads, autonomy may degenerate into a mechanism of repression and supression. Therefore, at present, autonomy is not a life and death questbn for the universities. A hundred times more urgent question at issue is the problem of their survival with grace, dignity and excellence. Therefore, they must be led by scruplous people having open minds and large hearts.

Autonomy is not an unvulnerable concept. Scholars, and administrators have disputed it, and are still disputing even in a developed country like USA. In our own country, the late renowned academician and administrator Dr.R.K. Singh maintained that it is in the interest of the universities to give an early 'farewel' to the fiction of autonomy from their campuses. "Autonomy in the sense of full self-governance", observed Carnegie Commission (1973), "does not exist for American Higher Education, nor has it existed for a very long time if ever. Autonomy is limited by the law, by the necessary influences and controls that go along with financial support, and by public policy in areas of substantial public concern. Autonomy in these areas is neither possible nor generally desirable." The Report of Commission further pointed out that in both North America and Western Europe, institutional independence is currently declining. T.N. Kaul (1988), who conducted research on governance of universities and autonomy of the university community, has reached to a similar conclusion. He is of the opinion that "no social institution which has a part to play in the preservation and promotion of a nation's culture and its development, and least of all university which trains the intelligence and moral fibre of society, can be independent. Indeed, independence without accountability may be inimical to the true and lasting interests of the universities, and....some universities administered by government department both in Europe and pre-independence India, managed to maintain substantial autonomy where it mattered most. A university need not loose its class or caste merely because of the restraints on its autonomy, such a restraint may actually signify greater concern of the society with its well being."

By and large, knowledgeable people agree that university autonomy has been betrayed and battered almost equally by the insiders and outsiders. In the insiders are included the teachers, students and the administrative staff; and in the outsiders the parents, politicians, government agencies and bureaucrats. Both the groups are guided by their self-interests in harming autonomy. Insiders inflict and diminish autonomy by their lack of institutional loyalty and professional commitment whereas the outsiders coerce and curtail autonomy through their office to seek undue favours and personal gains. Politicians and bureaucrats mostly devitalize and undermine university's independence by back-stage manipulation. Anyone who refuses to carry out the wishes of the power lords is sooner or later put in his place. He either quits himself or made to quit by humiliation and harrassment. Very often, in day-to-day functioning, university-autonomy is violated starting from admissions of students, allocation of specialization and examination results to the appointments of teachers and administrative staff. Even the staff of Chancellor's office do not hesitate to extract benefits from the university. Ministers of Central Government have been found to influence the process of appointments, and inquiry proceeding conducted in the universities. Indeed, "political patronage and intervention from behind the scene", says Amrik Singh, (1984), "is a real menace to the university, for the way the political bosses work is insiduous as well as invisible. The whole thing is bound up with the ethos of public life. We have seen it deteriorate over the years and universities are one of the institutions that have suffered as a result of this degeneration in the norms of political conduct."

With some 'ifs' and 'buts', here and there, almost all enlightened people accept that the institutions which "stand for humanism, for tolerance, for reason, for adventure of ideas and for the search of truth (Nehru, 1947)" must be granted autonomy in their governance. Otherwise they will not be able to discharge their duties and responsibilities truthfully and objectively. In Cardinal Newman's (1947), words, "universities have been entrusted with still greater social responsibilities of raising the intellectual tone of the society, of cultivating the public mind, of purifying the material taste, of supplying true principles, to popular enthusiams and fixed aims to popular aspiration, of giving enlargement and soberiety to the ideas of the age, of facilitating the exercise of political power, and refining the intercourse of private life." In point of fact, the professors teach, do research and through their activities define the university. Their work, is in essence, the university. Autonomy and obligations of university, therefore, automatically become the autonomy and obligations of the professoriate. In order to exercise, promote and preserve self-governance in the universities, they must equip themselves with high standard of conduct, intellectual alacrity and moral courage. It is equally important to create internal democracy and team spirit inside the university before the idea of autonomy is put into practice.

Almost complete collapse and breakdown of the system of higher education in the country has pricked the conscience of the educated people at large. In spite of widespread digust, anguish and disappointment with the system, the academic community is seen unwilling to think in a dedicated manner to salvage the university system, and to make it a real 'republic of scholars' and a 'kingdom of mind' through rediscovery and rehabilitation of self-governance. At this juncture, we must pay attention to a timely warning advanced by late J.D. Sethi (1983): "Neutrality and objectivity are value free and presume a certain amount of lack of commitment. This is no longer acceptable or even desirable. Certain clearcut objectives, norms and values have to be clearly delineated, accepted and practised if higher education is to be saved."

Having diagnosed the theoretical and practical aspects of autonomy of universities, I feel inclined to put my finger on the 'performance syndrome' of universities. Infact, performance is the culmination and distillation of all the inputs and efforts invested in a university. It is also known as the quest and the conquest of a university. To our utmost discomfort, excepting a few, majority of the universities could not put forth excellent performance. A large number of their products are unemployable, and perhaps this gives a reason to call them the 'wastelands' of higher education. Nothing can give universities more glamourous support and disarming argument for their autonomy than an outstanding or world-class performance. This is an adequate ground to give them credibility and to mobilize public opinion in favour of their self-governance, warding off unfair and undue influence and intervention from all sides. Though they have single faculties, the example or model of self-governance of IITs and IIMs is worthy of emulation for the universities to safeguard their autonomy. Another ingredient which can be helpful to strengthen their independence is their social commitment. A bridge between gown and town or university and city has to be built to enrich the experiences of the university community on the one hand, and to share the hardships and concerns of the larger community on the other. The universities should act as 'clearing houses' of information and expert knowledge for the society. The professoriate and the students should come out of the cocoon of the university to help the people to solve their problems, and thus increase their copability.

The academicians and scholars can use the society as a laboratory to test and apply the findings of their research and deliberation. At present, the universities are largely elitist in their approach and attitude and hence there is very little space left for the needs, aspirations and welfare of the masses. It will not be an overstatement to say in the end, that the real issue in the immediate context, is not "autonomy Vs Government or politicians', but "autonomy Vs accountability', since every failure is a failure of moral commitment to the mission and the people.

## References

Amrik Singh, *Asking for Trouble: What it means to be a Vice-Chancellor*. Delhi: Vikas Publishing House, 1984.

Ashby, Sir Eric, *The Bulletin of International Association of universities*, Nov. 1962.

Goheen, Robert, *The Human Nature of a University*, 1969.

Kaul, J.N., *Governance of Universities: Autonomy of University-Community*, Delhi: Abhinav Publications, 1988.

Nehru, J.L., *Convocation Address*, Allahabad University, 1947.

Newman, J.H. Cardinal, *The Idea of a University*, New York: Longman Green and Co., 1947.

*Report of the Education Commission* (1964-66), Delhi : Ministry of Education, 1966.

*Report of the Committee on Governan of Universities and Colleges*, Delhi: U.G.C., 1971.

*Report of the Carnegie Commission on Governance of Higher Education*, New Yorks McGraw Hill, 1973.

Sethi, J.D., *The Crisis and Collapse of Higher Education in India*, Delhi: Vikas Publishing House, 1983.

# 7

# University : An Oasis of Intellectual Life*

There are very few authors and speakers in whose writings and speeches one is feasted with a beautiful blending of religion and science, East and West, and tradition and modernity. Late Dr. S. Radhakrishnan is one of them. The more you read his books, the more unread you become. Since he was an educator *par excellence,* it is highly rewarding for a teacher to read his work intensively and comprehensively.

His book: *The Creative Life,* though first published in 1975, is very much relevant and illuminating even today, in the times of moral inertia and spiritual vacuum. In this book, Dr. Radhakrishnan is seen almost distressed at the sight of divisive, destructive and degenerative activities in which the human beings are involved. They have reduced the society to a "disorganized dust of individuals". Growing brutalization, vulgarization and robotization of men constrained him to say that "man has ceased to be a creative person". But, even this saddening scenario does not diminish his faith in man's creative potential. In the chapter on 'Growing Interdependence' his eulogy for men is worth noticing'.

---

* Review of Dr. S. Radhakrishnan's book : *The creative life.*

"What man has achieved so far is immense, yet it is very small compared to what he may yet achieve. History has many surprises in store for us."

Dr. Radhakrishnan through his persuasive pen, urges mankind to achieve completeness of being through rigorous discipline of mind and chastity of spirit for the purpose of producing a better and creative life in which every man will have more amplitude of existence, more richness of being and more fervour of friendship.

As regards the purpose of education, he insists that the kind of education that is imparted must not only be broad but should also be deep. True education should give not merely smattering of learning and skills but endow an individual with a definite purpose in life, defined by himself or herself. In agreement with our great tradition, he advocates the study of our great classics and communion with great minds. To rise above the level of human animal, it is essential for every human being to develop the quality of considerateness, kindness and compassion.

We must set for ourselves the straight goal of commitment to knowledge and advancement of learning by making our contributions to the great adventures which are taking place in this world. Our knowledge must equip us with the power to overcome spiritual stagnation and foster spiritual sensitivity. Education worth its name, must free us from all prejudices and presuppositions and look upon all as Kith and Kin. A truely liberating education is a second birth, a renewal.

Dr. Radhakrishnan asserts that man as a logical being is not a final end in human evolution. His logical mind has to grow into spiritual fill up the 'inner vacuum' created by our undue emphasis on materialism and sciencism reducing human beings to 'creatures of comfort'. We are, therefore, called upon to use all the resources available to us for the purpose of perfecting ourselves. An objective study of scientific truth means an intellectual excellence, moral excellence and emotional commitment.

Science and religion represent two dimensions to the human being : the rational and the spiritual. If a human being is to become really human, science and religion must be integrated. On deeper scrutiny, we may realize that science and technology, if they establish anything, establish the omnipotence of the human spirit and not the omnipotence of matter.

While elucidating the concept of an 'Ideal University" Dr. Radhakrishnan propounds that the university is the sanctuary of the intellectual life of the country. When we impart education we start a ferment of debate and discussion of first principles. The educated youth will voice their thoughts and find fault with things as they are. We train in the universities not only doctors and engineers but also men and women who think for themselves. They will not judge everything by the party line. If we destroy the initiative, the freedom of the people, we do so at our peril. If men lose intellectual vigour, the future of civilization is bleak indeed. The students of university should be trained to struggle against ignorance, injustice, operession and fear. It is the function of a teacher not to give pupils what they want but make them want what he gives them.

Human beings today are divided, riven and discordant personalities. Unless they are able to overcome evil and integrate their own nature, they will not be able to have any kind of insight into fundamental reality. In other words, the inward and the outward must cohere and must go together. It is only then that we can call ourselves humen beings, fulfilled human beings, not merely incomplete human beings as we happen to be. For this integration to take place, a symbiosis of time-tested traditional values and modern knowledge is necessary. The ideas and ideals may be the same but skills and techniques have been changing from age to age. We must reckon with this modern challenge.

Dr. Radhakrishnan appears to feel deeply concerned about removing the roots of evil and, the forces which are destroying the good that we have. He reproduces the statement of one of the characters created by the Roman playwright Terence in which he said : "I am a human being, so there is nothing human that is not my concern". The author defines 'peace' as the harmonizing of men in their differences, it is giving battle to distrust and prejudice. Thus viewed, peace, international understanding and human reconciliation are synonymous, since the rise of force and ooercion in settling differences and conflicts is not only bad morals but is bad policy as well. The intense nationalism of today has to give place to a true internationalism. A new man has to be created who feels for humanity as a whole. This change in man required inward change.

"In a university", Dr. Radhakrishnan emphasizes, "it is given to us to learn from one another, learn about one another, about other people's beliefs, about othor people's practices, bring about an understanding of one another. All the religions, all the cultures, all the civilizations will come together one day. And this gives us an opportunity to see that though there may not be uniformity, there may be harmony, there may be unity, there may be recognition that all are parties in the one supreme task of nourishing the spiritual life of mankind, and not rivals for power, for domination. 'We must, therefore, try to understand and appreciate each other, and recognize them as good or as bad as ourselves. That is what all academies and universities stand for. A kind of intellectual cooperation and solidarity is also essential for stabilizing the new emerging world which has been created by the contribution of people of all countries, creeds and complexions.

# 8

# Imagination and University Education

In fact, a university is imagination or it is nothing, at least nothing useful. The justification for a university, in the opinion of the eminent philosopher - mathematician, A. N. Whitehead, is that it preserves the connection between knowledge and zest for life, by connecting the young and the old in the imaginative consideration of learning. The university imparts information, but it imparts it imaginatively. A university which fails in this respect has no reason for existence.

Education is discipline for the adventure of life. Research is intellectual adventure, and, therefore universities should be homes of adventure shared in common by the young and old. For successful higher education there must always be a certain freshness in the knowledge dealt with. It must either be new in itself or it must be invested with some novelty of application to the new world or the new times.

The climate of excitement, arising from imaginative consideration, transforms knowledge. A fact no more remains a bare fact. It is invested with all its possibilities. It is no longer a burden on the memory. It is energising "as the poet of our dreams, and as the architect of our purposes". Thus, human imagination has the potential to bring about a mutation in the life of the mind.

Imagination is not separable from the facts. Really speaking, it is a way of illuminating facts. It works by eliciting the general principles which apply to the facts, as they exist, and then by an intellectual survey of alternative possibilities which are consistent with those principles. It enables men to construct an intellectual vision of a new world, and it also preserves the zest for life by the suggestion of satisfying purposes.

Youth is not defined by years but by the creative impulse and drive to make something different. During the school period the student has been mentally bending over his desk. At the university he should stand up and look around to raise doubts and questions. Youth is imaginative, and if the imagination be strengthened by discipline, this energy of imagination can in great measure be preserved through life. "The tragedy of the world is", Whitehead laments, that "those who are imaginative have but slight experience, and those who are experienced have feeble imaginations. Fools act on imagination without knowledge; pedants act on knowledge without imagination. The task of university is to weld together imagination and experience".

The initial discipline of imagination in its period of youthful vigour requires that there be no responsibility for immediate action. The habit of unbiased thought, whereby the ideal variety of exemplifications is discerned in its derivation form general principles, can not be acquired when there is the daily task of preserving a concrete organization. One must be free to think rightly or wrongly, and free to appreciate the variousness of the universe undisturbed by distractions and perils.

Imagination can not be delivered to the students by their teachers in measured or weighed quantity. It can only be communicated by a faculty whose member themselves wear learning with imagination. The whole art in the organization of a university is the provision of a faculty whose learning is lighted up with imagination. This is the 'problem of problems' of the university education. Unless we are careful, the recent vast explosion of universities in number of students and in variety of activities, of which we are so justly proud, will fail in producing results, by mishandling of this problem.

The combination of learning and imagination normally requires some leisure, freedom from restraint, freedom from harassing worries, some variety of experiences, and the stimulation of other minds diverse in opinion and diverse in equipment. Also there is required the excitement of curiosity and the self - confidence derived from pride in the achievements of the surrounding society in procuring the advancement of knowledge. Imagination can not be acquired once and for all, and then kept indefinitely in an ice box to be produced periodically in stated quantities. The learned and imaginative life, is a way of living, and is not an 'article of commerce'.

It is in respect to the provision and utilization of these conditions for an efficient faculty that the two functions of education and research meet together in a university. If we want our teachers to be imaginative, then encourage them to do research. If we want our researchers to be imaginative, then bring theme into intellectual sympathy with the young at the most eager, imaginative period of life when intellects are just entering upon their mature discipline.

Professors ought to be people put on perfection, bubbling with excitement for ideas. They should read, write and speak great thoughts. They should try to hitch their wagon to the highest star. The faculty should be a band of scholars stimulating each other, and freely determining their various activities. The whole point of a university, on its educational side, is to bring the young under the intellectual influence of a band of imaginative scholars. There can be no escape from proper attention to the condition which, as experience has shown, will produce such a band.

The proper function of a university is the imaginative acquisition of knowledge. Imagination is a contagious disease. It is the lighted torch which passes from hand to hand. It is a dangerous gift which has started many a conflagration. If we are timid as to that danger, the proper course is to shut down our universities, because timid people (professors) and great universities cannot go together.

# 9

# University: A Sanctuary of Dissenting Ideas

Robert Goheen in his book: *The Human Nature of a University* (1969) asks an interesting question: "Where in your society can a person disagree with impunity from accepted practices, dogmas and doctrines ?" He himself gives the answer: "It is in the university". Infact, a university is a sanctuary of 'free inquiry' and an incubator of ideas-ideas of all variety and complexion. Universities are expected to engage themselves in the pursuit of truth and excellence in all its diversity. This is a pursuit which needs, above all, courage and fearlessness. Great universities and timid people can hardly go together.

A university must do at least two things to think of itself as a real university. Firstly, seek the truth and secondly, defend those who try to tell the truth under institution's auspices. If an institution tries to shrink from adhering to these two principles, it ceases to be a university, in spite of its grand achievements in all other areas of its functioning.

Really speaking, a university is a 'mega classroom', that is hospitable to hundreds of ideas of different parentage and persuasions. Teachers teach here to create space in which the 'community of truth' is practiced. Truth is weighed more than the truth seeker and teaching more than the teacher. Here, truth is considered as an 'eternal conversation' about things that matter, and conducted with passion and discipline. Good teaching, irrespective of its form, help more and more people learn to speak and listen in the community of truth to understand that truth is not in conclusion, so much as in the process of conversation itself. The conversation of truth can and must be internal as well as external. Internally it is called creative or intuitive thinking.

For many of us who teach, our fear of public conflict is a major barrier to creating space where the community of truth can be practiced. If we want to remove the barrier, we must help our students to know that conflict can be a paradoxical path to harmony and health for persons and groups. Many people are inclined to see conflict as terminal rather than creative because of their past association with the settings that are more competitive than consensual. In competition, the purpose of conflict is to determine which few will win at the expenses of the many. In consensus or creative dialogical mode, however, every one can win through conflict as the clash of apparent opposites gives rise to fresh and fuller truth.

A consensual or dialogical classroom assumes that truth requires plurality of voices and views, much speaking and listening and a high degree of tolerance for ambiguity in the midst of tenacious community. Consensual truth is not the outcome of majority vote. It is continuing revelation that appears as we air our differences in public, pay special attention to those who disagree, and seek deeper insight. Since, agreed upon truth is the only truth we have, it is vital that students be brought into process and into the conflict it contains.

The most important thing a teacher can do to encourage classroom dissension is to make the classroom a hospitable place. Only then are students likely to do the hard work on which the act of consensus-making depends. This includes exposing one's ignorance, challenging another's facts and interpretations, claiming one's own truth publicly and making vulnerable to the scrutiny of others. This is how a university can earn a privilege of a 'testing track' of competive and conflicting ideas.

John Dewey has said that the dominant mode of teaching followed in the colleges and universities turns education into a 'spectator sport'. It is an act of faithful rendering of objectivist epistemology. It keeps the knower at arm's length from the known so that subjective biases will not distort our knowledge. Reformers have rallied against this pedagogy because it holds the subjectivity at bay by keeping the students or youth off the field. This type of non-participative teaching makes learning passive and joyless, and turns too many educated people into 'spectators of life'.

The singular mission of the university will continue to be the creation of an autonomous public space that fosters creative dialogue to impart cultural, democratic and technocratic citizenship to students. "The university", says Gerald Delanty, "is a key institution of modernity and is the site where knowledge, culture and society inter-connect". It provides the structures for public debate between expert and lay cultures. This is how the university can evolve a new identity in the global age.

Scholars and academics of the university have an extra-ordinary responsibility to identify and challenge the enemies of open society. When the system gets extremely capitalistic or communistic, this has to be questioned. If it tends to be too much religious this too can be countered. If human beings combine to be exceedingly anthropocentric at the expense of biotic world, this should be resisted by creating a counter culture. The problem of globalization is that it is caught in the cult of managerialism and commodification of art, culture and education. The moral and ethical concerns are, therefore, lost on the road to economism.

# 10

# Virtual Universities or Digital Diploma Mills

Education is a social process. It processes both information and the people. Hence, human relationship is a basic requirement of educational transactions and interactions. The dramatic influence of human personality of a teacher can not be replaced by a robot or a TV tube. Empathic warmth and breath of life are communicable to the learners only by the loving presence of an affectionate teacher. Increasing use of technology and internet for imparting instruction in the distance education mode, has led to the erosion of "face-to-face pedagogy". By making the delivery of knowledge a commercial transaction in the virtual universities, the educational process has been rendered as much lifeless as a commodity. Thus, the commoditization of instruction has deprofessionalized the professoriate. Emphasizing the immense value of "face-to-face" transaction of curriculum, McDermott (2004) has observed that "for me, teaching is a response to the most fundamental of all human questions: 'can you help me ?'. I believe that we can see the existential urgency of this question in the faces before us, given, of course, that we remain face-to-face".

With the use of internet technologies, distance education has taken on new meaning as the 'virtual university". As of

November 2002, Phoenix university on-line has a staff of some 1,700 with some 7000 faculty - mostly part-time, teaching some 49,400 students. Phoenix has reported a net income of $ 64.3 million for the year 2001. There are number of companies and so called private on-line universities that have monopolized the area of distance education. They have almost overtaken traditional universities. These new commercial universities are pejoratively known as 'digital diploma mills' in Europe and America. American research-studies have revealed that, in majority of the cases, these virtual universities have no classrooms. Faculties are often untrained and part time or non-existent, and the officers are unethical self-seekers whose qualifications are no better than their offerings.

In his book: *Digital Diploma Mills*, David F. Noble (2002) has remarked that "the ambitious reach of today's distance educators is determinedly global in scale, which is why the World Trade Organization (WTO) is currently at work trying to remove any and all barriers of international trade in educational commodities.....Even it fails to deliver on its economic and pedagogical promises, as it surely will, its promoters will push it forward, nevertheless, given the investment entailed, leaving a legacy of corruption and ruin in its wake.". The WTO regime has been fully implemented with effect from January 1, 2005. Under General Agreement on Trade and Services (GATS), higher education will become a borderless service to be provided by the private and foreign institutions in any country through the four modes: distance education, E-learning, maximum use of Information and Communication Technology (ICT) and using Internet facilities.

It is very obvious, says Noam Chomsky, that "in the times of globalization world affairs are conducted according to the hegemonic good will or hierarchy of economic interest of the first world." From the position of strength and preparedness US and Europe have been pleading through the platform of WTO to ensure free flow of higher education between nations so that they can float educational companies and extend the campus of their universities in other countries. The WTO protocols and general agreements are aimed at commercialization of higher education and therefore they should be seen as threats to the concept, function and core values of autonomy and academic freedom in the university.

The universities have been established in the developing countries to meet their specialized academic aspirations, to contribute to national development and modernization of the society. This social mission of the universities will be greatly hampered by the WTO's philosophy of 'market fundamentalism'. The complexion of the academic institutions will be altered and the university culture will be colonized by the culture of capitalism. They will get reduced to the level of corporations like Enron and Tyco noted for their fraudulent practices and unethical accounting. The only way out to confront this competitive situation is to get quickly prepared by integrating quality, morality, creativity and professionalism with the ethos of the universities and colleges to make them world-class institutions.

It appears that post-secondary education is now a massive globalizing industry, and it is perhaps not possible at present to estimate its potential and promise. Asia alone offers a fantastic possibility. It is projected that by 2010, there will be 100 million people in the world, all fully qualified to proceed from secondary to tertiary education, but perhaps, there will be no rooms left on any campus. A recent study, made by Merrill Lynch reported that higher education market outside the USA would be worth $ 111 billion annually with about 32 million potential students. This raises more questions than it answers, especially regarding the possible consequence for the future of higher education.

A large number of professors are of the opinion that, though the brick or traditional universities face challenges of competition from the virtual or click universities, they are not going to disappear. Education will not be eclipsed entirely, but it is feared that higher education, due to its higher cost, will become largely an enclave of the rich and the powerful section of the society. To ensure quality in higher education, the second channel (on line) higher education needs to be regulated and coerced to play its academic role obeying the rules of the game and to ensure availability of adequate resources and inputs. Otherwise, a dismal new era of higher education will emerge for the disadvantaged and underprivileged. The virtual university should not be allowed to promote separation of knowledge production from knowledge dissemination function of the universities by exclusively associating itself with the task of teaching or knowledge dissemination. No higher education institution can claim the status of a university unless it genuinely gets involved in conducting research and initiating innovations to expand the horizons of knowledge and ideas.

# 11

# Educational Administrators and Challenges of the Future

So long as a society is relatively stable and unchanging, the problems it present to men tend to be routine and predictable. Organizations and institutions in such an environment can be relatively permanent. But when change is accelerated, more and more novel first-time problems arise, traditional forms of organization prove inadequate to the new conditions. They can no longer cope. In this situation, we need to create "self-destroying organizations." Traditional functional organization structures created to meet predictable, non-novel conditions prove in-capable of responding effectively to radical changes taking place in the environment.

**Self- Renewal**

When, John Gardner became secretary of Health, Education and Welfare in U.S.A. in 1965 a top to bottom re-organization shook the department. In his small book *Self-Renewal*, long before he entered the government, Gardner observed that "the far sighted administrator...... reorganizes to break down calcified organizational lines. He shifts personnel.....

He redefines jobs to break them out of rigid categories". Elsewhere Gardner referred to the "Crises of Organization" in government and suggested that, in both the public and private sectors, " most organizations have a structure that was designed to solve problems that no longer exist." The "self-renewing" organizations, he defined as are that constantly change in structure in response to changing needs. Organizational change or "self-renewal" as Gardner (1963) puts it, is a necessary, an unavoidable response to the acceleration of change.

"A developing society" observes Pascale and Athos (1982) "requires departure, change and novelty in language, in concepts and in ways of doing things. There has to be creative movement, at least at fairly frequent intervals." A society in a changing environment is doomed if it does not produce managerial/administrative innovations which break inherited mould of perception, old pattern of behaviour and prior expression of beliefs and values.

The traditional bureaucratic design of organization/ institutions has produced spineless, faceless "organization man". As a result of change, novelty and transience bureaucracy would take the shape of "ad-hocracy" and "organization man" will become "associative man", man having close, though temporary, relationships with the fellow workers and associates. The very temporariness with the organization frees him from many of the bonds that constricted his predecessor. Transience as *Toffler* (1970) says, is liberating.

"Ad-hocracy" would demand a different constellation of human characteristics. In place of permanence, transience and high mobility between organizations, never ending re-organizations within them, and a constant generation and decay of temporary work groupings. In such situation the man periodically examines his own attitude towards the organization and gauges its attitude towards him. If he does not like what he sees, he tries to change. If he can not change it, he moves. What John Gardner opined "the loyalty of the professional man is to his profession and not to organization that may house him at any given moment." The introduction of Ad-hocracy would increase the adaptability of organization; but it strains the adaptability of men. Frequent adaptations are made at the cost of personal satisfaction and adjustment. Adhocracy means a sharp acceleration in the turn-over of organizational relationship in his life. The increased turn-over of all these relationships place a heavy adaptive burden on individuals reared and educated for life in slower-paced social system of developing countries.

**Paradigm shifting**

Transition is taking place from, namely, "more of the same" and "better than before" to "different than before" stage. To deliver the goods in the organizations and institutions, the third stage requires "frame breakers" or "paradigm shifters".

A paradigm shifter is some one who throws out the rules of the game and institutes radical, not incremental change—a leader who foments revolution, not evolution. Noel Tichy, the University of Michigam business Professor, says that "incrementally fixing the old broken bureaucracy just is not doing the job these days. What is required are quantum ideas for products and services, as well as revolutionary changes in the organization to produce them. General Electric Chief Executive Officer and ultimate paradigm shifter Jack Welch adds: "It is not just quantum ideas, but the guts to stick with them."

Paradigm shifting has become a management fad in the United States. As Tichy points out: this is not just some cute little gimmick. It is difficult, it is painful, and it involves a fundamental shift in a corporation, including power. Consequently, the ugly truth is that real paradigm shifting rarely occurs within traditional Corporation or organization. And when it does, individual paradigm shifters-usually tenacious, highly opinionated, action-oriented types whose speciality is, after all, rocking the corporate boat-often don't survive the process.

John Trani, the Welch lieutenant who over-hauled and run GE Medical Systems, says that "Growth the way we did it is not easy. Change is never easy when you do it on multiple fronts. But the organization that adapts itself continuously will win, and for that you have to have leaders and managers who love change. Paradigms do not shift by thinking about them. At best, the plan is 20 per cent of the game. Execution is 80 per cent of it." Pick the right people, Allocate the resources, Build the organization's Competency and, share the information and decision load are some of the imperatives of paradigm shifting (Toffler,1991).

For a real paradigm shift to occur within an institution or organization, "there has to be divine discontent with the status quo at the very top, and the courage to do something about it says Ram Charan, a consultant to many *Fortune 500* corporations and a former Havard Business School Faculty member. At the same time, Charan cautions executives to stop looking to academic management fads for solutions. Instead, he insists that give the customers what they want and need. Get the quality that is required. Achieving continuous improvement in productivity and making decisions and executing them is the real name of the game (Huey, 1992).

**Bridging spiritual and institutional life**

Western societies evolved separate institutions with separate spheres of influence. The Church emerged as custodian of man's faith and spiritual life. On the other hand, governmental and commercial institutions were given the role of providing for man's worldly existence. Western organization theory evolved to legitimize this duality as a natural state of affairs. Machiavelli in the sixteenth century was one of the first to consider administration as a function separate from moral laws. He advanced an amoral theory of governing organizations.

Later on, ascendency given to bureaucratic institution, by Max Weber reinforced the view expressed by Machiavelli. In Weber's writings on organizations, factors like size, complexity, formalization and centralization were discussed and emphasized. In fact, those factors still remain principal dimensions along which we still think about organizational designs.

Although, Eastern societies never favoured separation of man's spiritual life from his institutional yet their prolonged domination by the West, and particularly by the Britishers had its impact on their institutions and organizations. Since China and Japan did not suffer the pangs of colonization by Western rulers for a longer time, these countries could maintain spiritual tradition in their institutions and organization.

In Eastern societies spiritual, public and private matters were so integrated that their organizations tended to regard the task of control in the context of the whole of human needs, rather than as a more narrow transaction between labour and Capital. They were generally more sophisticated than the West in utilizing social and spiritual forces for the organizational benefit, and in accepting the responsibilities to their employees that went with such broad influence. A return to this bridging of spiritual and institutional lives has become necessary to offset increasing dehumanization and valuelessness in the educational institutions and organizations.

**Mccting the Demands of New Roles**

The 21st century, unlike any other period in our history, will offer major challenges to our human resources capacities as we enter a period of rapid social, technological and economic change. We can expect such fluctuations and upheavals to progress at an even more accelerated rate in the next century. Keeping up with societal changes will consume much energy and require unusual resourcefulness on the part of most of Indians and inhabitants of other countries.

Life transitions challenge people and require them to grow and adapt to meet the demands of new roles. This is the environment that explains the widespread participation of adults in education and it will explain their continued large scale participation in education in the years ahead. Therefore, "our people must be knowledgeable, as well as trained, as competent, and as inventive as those in any other nations. All of our people, not just a few must be able to think for a living, adapt to changing environments, and to understand the world around them. They must understand and accept the responsibilities and obligations of citizenship. They must continually learn and develop new skills throughout their lives. We must recognize that education is a life long pursuit, not just an endeavour for our children (Aslanian, 1992)". This agenda of the "National Goals for Education" put forward by the White House, is the greatest challenge of the future facing the educational administrators of all the countries of the world.

## References

Aslanian, Carol B. (1992) Adults on campus. *Span*. XXXIII (6) 12-13, June.

Gardner, John (1963) *Self-Renewal*. Evanstion, Illinois : Harper.

Huey, John (1992) Nothing is impossible. *Span*. XXXIII(6), p. 7, June.

Fascale, Richard Tanner and Athos, Anthony G. (1982). *The Art of Japanese Management*. New York : Warner Books.

Toffler, Alvin (1971) *Future shock*. London: Pan Books Ltd.

Toffler, Alvin (1991) *Power Shift*. New York: Bantam Books.

# 12

# Educational Administrator: An Entrepreneur and Incubator of Ideas

Educational administration is the process and agency of integrating the efforts of personnel, and of utilizing appropriate material and ideas in such a way as to promote effectively the development of human quality. The new concept of administration puts less emphasis on the administrator having specialized competence in all aspects of educational activity, and more stress on his possession of broad general professional competence coupled with highly developed skills in the areas of human relation and administrative processes.

Administration must necessarily take place in an interpersonal setting. The crucial factor in administration, therefore, is the nature of the human relationship involved. The administrator's basic functions are to exercise broad judgment, provide professional leadership and exhibit discriminating insight and understanding in the utilization of personnel. It is perhaps because of the perennial concern for promoting the 'human element' that the *Education commission* (1964-66) advocated educational administration to be a "matter of faith and vision, bold and courageous leadership and proper handling of human relationship". Thus, cooperative rather than manipulative approach has to be employed in eliciting the contribution of personnel to realize the organizational goals.

In education, administration would continue to be a service agency to teaching, research and extension work. One cannot be a good educational administrator unless one is a good teacher. Hence there should always be an opportunity open for an educational administrator to come back to teaching or research, and for a teacher to go over to the administrative side on a tenure assignment. Educational administration and teaching must draw inspiration, support and enrichment from each other through periodic exchange of roles. Studies on effective educational institutions have also reinforced the belief that an educational administrator must be a strong instructional leader. He should promote orderly climate in the institution, set high expectations for the students, put emphasis on basic skills and regularly monitor instructional progress of the learners.

In their now famous work *The Art of Japanese Management*, Pascale and Athos, while discussing the seven "Ss" of management, have drawn the conclusion that the western emphasis on the first three "Ss" (Strategy, Structure and Systems) has produced an arid world in which nothing is alive. "An organization is often given its life", they say, through the four soft "Ss", that is, Staff, Skill, Style and Super-ordinate goals". The astounding success of many japanese companies through meticulous attention to the soft "Ss", which act as a lubricant in the organization machine to keep the hard "Ss" from grinding one another away. To utilize and mobilize human energy and creativity through harmonious human relationships, the educational administrators must orient themselves to the demands of the four soft "Ss".

Today, competition poses an organizational challenge that can not be met simply by technology or financial resources, Technological innovations and resource allocation are outcomes of human processes, therefore, our ability to compete rests on our ability to organize human beings in such a way as to generate opportunity and results rather than impasses, stagnation, bureaucracy and wasteful friction. Interpersonal relations and dialogue, therefore, have to be recognized as the basic ingredients of educational administration to enable people to come together, to keep together and to work together for generating new ideas and strategies needed for organizational change.

In an educational organization highly educated people work and Interact. The more educated a population, the more democracy and openness it seems to demand. A more educated group can not be managed in the traditional authoritarian "don't ask me a question" fashion. Infact, asking questions and challenging assumptions are becoming part of everybody's Job. Novelty and Originality will not emerge In an organization unless such protestant attitude prevails there, "The more the society advances towards a super-symbolic economy", observes Alvin Toffler, "the more important it becomes to permit an extremely wide range of dissent and free expression. The more any government chokes off or chills this rich, free flow of data, information, and knowledge including wild ideas, innovation, and even political dissent the more it slows down the advance of the new economy".

Educational institutions are not surrogate machines like the "robots" which do not rebel. They are the abodes of culture where spirit of inquiry, questioning and disagreement are deliberately fostered. Here the people should disagree without being disagreeable, and value substantive conflict, by keeping personal conflict to a minimum. To usher in such a permissive intellectual climate, an educational administrator is expected to possess democratic attitude, scientific temper and philosophic tolerance to play a role of an incubator of ideas. Administrators having such a mind-set and temperament of an entrepreneur can make an educational institution a true "academic republic" and an intellectual enterprise.

The human beings are ordained with two opposing propensities: the urge to create and he urge to destroy. They also exhibit the tendency to shirk and dodge as well as the capacity to work hard and excel. Human beings do not like to stay simply as creatures of God. They frequently strive to be creators. But when the urge to create and excel is thwarted, urge to destroy comes into play. Hence it is a major responsibility of an educational administrator to create such conditions and contexts, in the educational institution, that stimulate and inspire the teachers to perform at qualitatively better and higher level. They should also make attempts to develop in the teachers and educational workers a "life style", which in the words of A.N. whitehead, 'hates waste, economises material and prefers good work".

The 21st century, unlike any other period in our history, will offer major challenges to human resources capacities as we enter a period of rapid social, technological and economic change. We can expect many disorienting fluctuations and upheavals in the path of progress at an even more accelerated rate in the future. To regulate societal changes for better tomorrow will consume much energy and require unusual resourcefulness and imagination on the part of the educational leaders. Preparedness, openness and readiness for renewal are the characteristics that the educational administrators are required to absorb, to enable educational organizations and institutions to be fit for facing uncertainties and emergencies originating from premature arrival of the future.

# 13

# Under Performance and Indifference of Teachers in Higher Education

In the past two decades, under-performance and indifference of teachers towards students has come under severe criticism. People have gone to the extent of saying that teachers of universities and colleges get "full salary for half work". This observation is not wholly devoid of substance, yet majority of the teachers have reacted to it very sharply. They say that singling out teaching profession for under-performance is an attempt to scandalize and malign teachers in the eyes of larger public. Some young teachers and students think that our academics are doing good work in some Indian Universities and abroad. One student, of social science, studying at Cambridge, has noted that "today India is to academic research what the NICs are to consumer goods. And not just in terms of the number of academic papers published. If almost 80 per cent of all consumer goods sold in Western supermarkets have been made in East Asia, at least 50 percent of all papers referred to by the students of my course were written by 'Indians still working in India." But, these are the exceptions which do not make the rule.

It is always thought good for the academic health of the country to occasionally bring into open and dissect teachers' performance and achievement. But, ringing the bell of under-performance and non-performance incessantly into the ears of the public would ultimately generate a feeling of cynicism, diffidence and worthlessness in the teachers. This type of wholesale cursing and condemning approach not only demoralizes the teaching community, but brings the whole system of education and its auxiliary agencies into great disrepute.

The purpose of writing this article is not to defend under-performance but to highlight those conditions and causes which impinge upon the teachers to gradually render them dull, insensitive, unaspiring and finally to paralyse their capacity and drive to perform. Performance is not an independent variable. It is not always within the control of an individual to perform according to his wishes or according to theoretical prescription. What matters most is the reality in which a worker is enveloped in the work-situation.

Performance is directly proportional to the situation, context and climate of the institution or organization. Researches have shown that monotonous and uninspiring context has a retarding influence on performance and achievement. Poor conditions of work and lack of facilities contribute to under-performance. Closed and direct organizational climate stifles initiative, spontaneity and innovativeness.

Let me now try to critically examine the scenario of our higher educational institutions. It is no exaggeration to say that nearly 40 per cent, of around 18,000 colleges in our country are economically unviable. Many of them are owned by the politicians who oblige, the party in power, at the time of election. Universities are also opened, under political pressure, without obtaining prior sanction from the UGC, and without even meeting the minimum requirements. Such institutions which are opened to serve political ends, hardly bother to abide by the laid down academic norms, for years, and thus conduce to lowering of standards. In such institutions, teachers' under-performance is inevitable. Thus, the most potent and cogent factor responsible for under-performance by the teachers is the political patronage and interference. Would the teachers' organizations come forward to keep the educational institutions free from the corrosive influence of political parties in general, and from providing political parenthood to incompetent teachers in particular. In most of the cases performance and accountability depend upon the type of the people recruited to the profession. We need competent; creative and caring teachers. Somebody has beautifully said that "teaching resembles gardening except for the propensity to lecture to the roses". We really need to recruit teachers who possess the warmth and affection to make the roses bloom.

Unfortunately, these days, experts who sit on the selection committees, give too much weightage to research degree and publications, and they rarely bother for the attitude and inclination of the candidate towards teaching. In fact, teaching is not as much a matter of scholarship and research as it is of aptitude and attitude. Simply passing a test on morality would not make one a moral person. In the same way, getting through a national entrance test for teaching would rarely make a 55% postgraduate an effective and worthy teacher. Hence, a balance has to be struck between cognitive and affective demands of teaching, at the time of recruitment.

By this remark I do not mean to under-estimate the role of research in the area of higher education. As a matter of fact, research is an antidote to intellectual death. But in no way the glamour and snob-value arrogated to research activity be allowed to disturb the requisite balance between research and teaching. What is expected, in the interest of higher education, is to see that the input of research in teaching updates the teacher and enriches teaching.

We are aware of the academic havoc played by nearly one hundred odd private university in the state of Chhatisgarh. Today around 60% of the universities are suffering from lack of minimum teaching and research facilities. On the other hand, corruption is erupting in some of the universities like a volcano as financial discipline, professional commitment and ethical consideration are diminishing day by day.

The organizational climate of university departments and colleges is greatly responsible for under-performance by the teachers. Our colleges and universities are 'over-administered' and 'under-led'. The organizational (institutional) climate obtaining in most of the institutions is closed and autocratic. The reward structure, inside and outside the institutions, also militates against the genuine, silent and self-respecting teachers. Careerism is so rampant that, in order to climb up the ladder, many of the teachers are seen prepared to get exploited by the heads or the principals, at the earliest opportunity. They can be seen writing papers and books for the personal gain of the Head or the Principal. Instead of regarding the institution as a 'cooperative commonwealth' of all the employees, the Head or the Principal treats it as his/her 'Jageer'. As a result, sychophants and satellites mushroom, the tide of mediocrity rises, creativity gets stifled and pursuit of excellence takes a back seat. The management councils or governing bodies also play the role of a villain in the high drama of educational floundering.

A teacher cannot remain insulated and unaffected by the utilitarian and pragmatic milieu of the larger society. Like doctors and engineers, he also hankers after money and higher standards of living. Like the members of other occupations and professions, the teacher has also become partially blind to social commitment, values and ideals. Bureaucratization and commercialization of education have further prompted teachers to adopt a mechanical and money-centred attitude. Consequently, their role has been reduced to an extension of 'input-output process' of the system of education. Increasing use of media and technology in the classrooms has constricted their concern for and 'face-to-face' contact with the students. Touch and feel of life is gradually vanishing in the classrooms. The act of teaching remains no more a source of joy or a medium of self-expression for majority of teachers.

The human being is ordained with two opposing propensities: the urge to create, and the urge to destroy. Men also possess the tendency to shirk from the responsibility, as well as the capacity to work hard and excel. Human beings do not like to stay simply as creatures of God. They very often strive to be creators. But, when the urge to create and excel is thwarted, the urge to destroy comes into play. Hence, it is the major responsibility of the educational administrators and leaders to create such smart conditions and contexts in the institutions which stimulate and inspire teachers to perform qualitatively better and higher. In fact, there is no dearth of potentially competent and caring teachers in the institutions of higher education. What is lacking therein is the ability and imagination on the part of the administrators to enable the young teachers to actualize their potentialities.

# 14

# Teacher Education and Challenges of Change

In his recently published book *Tomorrow's Teachers*, Alan Scott of USA, made an analysis that production of new teachers has become a sharp political issue through out the world. Teacher education is coming under increasing attack from politicians, economists, parent organisations and social critic alike. At present, tension between liberal ideas and economic imperatives are pulling and pushing teacher education in contradictory direction. Educational ideas seem too readily and dogmatically to be treated for immediate fiscal policy. Such a shortsighted approach is detrimental to effective education.

In our country, in the recommendations of various commissions and committees on teacher education has been assigned a pivotal place. But in actual practice, it is languishing in unfavourable institutional setting for want of financial and political support. In contrast to other professional areas, it is treated even today as a poor relation. That is why, perhaps, it is said that "teacher education is a slum in the city of higher education."

To begin with, I would like to invite your attention to the following problems and issues with which the Indian institutions of teacher education are infested. These problems are old and new at the same time:

1. We witness isolation of colleges of education and university departments of education amongst themselves, and from other professional and general institutions of education. This situation prevents enrichment and cross fertilisation of ideas through interaction and synergy leading ultimately to stagnation and fossilization of teacher education.
2. The internal socio-psychological ethos is full of regimentation, and it suppresses free expression and questioning on the part of pupil-teachers. Thus, a bad model of teaching and administrative behaviour is presented before the prospective teachers. In this context, I am reminded of two sayings, which are in circulation among the teacher-trainees. One is "Keep your mouth closed and purse open," and the other one is "B.Ed. training is a rigorous imprisonment of nine months".
3. There is a lack of balance between theory and practice of teaching. The teacher-training programmes are more oriented towards theory. The teachers of teachers do not practice the methodology and approaches which they preach in the classrooms, and expect students to practice them. The practice of teaching neither is taken seriously nor is supervised sincerely and systematically. Simulated practice of teaching has degenerated into a dogma and mockery.
4. Governments are apathetic and indifferent to college of education in general, but in M.P., it has acquired a dangerous and destructive dimension. In almost all govt. colleges of education, a requisite 'set-up' for the colleges has not been implemented, and at present, these institutions are being run with the help of borrowed school teachers.

5. Teacher educators, in general, of course with honourable exceptions, lack initiative, enterprise and innovativeness. There is a felt need to raise the level of their competence to make them comparable with the professionals of other technical and professional institutions. They have to be made tech-savvy and aware of the 'paradigm shift' going on in almost all other areas.
6. Leadership of national institutes in the field of teacher-education is not vibrant and dynamic. NCERT, NCTE and NIEPA have been ritualised beyond imagination. So far, they have not been effective and successful in disseminating and percolating down researches, new knowledge, strategies and innovative practises to the last teacher.
7. Immediate efforts are needed to induct talent in the institutions of teacher education. At the same time, talent inside the institutions be encouraged and nurtured. Sociology of educational knowledge is changing, and therefore, there is an urgent need to develop teacher education institutions as centre of activity and creativity.
8. The third millennium has its own imperative to pursue. Firstly, it lays emphasis on competition. To survive in a competitive environment, teacher-education must update their knowledge, undertake quality research and introduce innovative practices and strategies in the institutions. Our preference for quality and excellence will go a long way in equipping us to fare better in a competitive situation. Similarly, an inclination to acquire training from time to time and to gain a sense of professionalism would sharpen the tools and techniques, and instil commitment to the profession.

We are living in the times of rapid change; in such transient times, a premium is put on teacher and teacher education to make the context copable for the youth to avoid 'crash landing' in the future. Students are needed a preparedness to face emergencies and uncertainties. Hence, the teacher's educators are expected to plan their teaching to inculcate flexible attitudes and receptivity to change in the learners. Creative approach to teaching and learning is the right remedy for the present malady.

A teacher is a telescope through which the people can see the distant tomorrows of the students and the country. The teachers are the moderators between the past and the future. They make the students aware of the limitation and value of the past. A competent and caring teacher can defeat time by speaking a right word and by communicating a bright idea to the students in the classroom.

We are living in an age of accelerating change and super complexity, which is straining our 'physical defences'and overwhelming our 'decisional processes'. In this situation, creative and committed teachers can help students and the community to subject the process of change and evolution to conscious human guidance for making imaginative use of change. Alvin Toffler has rightly observed: "By making imaginative use of change to channel change, we can not only spare ourselves the trauma of future shock, we can reach out and humanize distant tomorrows". In the times of radical uncertainty, the key educational challenge is not one of the 'knowledge' but of 'being', since super complexity can dislocate the self. Hence, to cope with the challenge of change, we need to evolve a 'therapeutic pedagogy' which offers a chance of recovering the 'self'. After all, the modern world needs not just competent teachers, but teachers who can question their own actions and who are able to envisage new forms of professionalism.

In the words of Parker J. Palmer, teaching "like any truly human activity, emerges from one's inwardness, for better or worse. As we teach we project the condition of our souls onto our students, our subjects and our ways of being together. The enlargements of one's experience in the classroom are often no more or less than convolutions of one's inner life. Viewed from this angle, teaching holds a mirror to the soul. If we are willing to look in that mirror, and not run from what we see, we have a chance to gain self knowledge; and knowing our-self is as crucial to good teaching as knowing our students and our subjects."

# 15

# Continuing Education of University and College Teachers

George, Z.F. Bereday has observed that a University is so many things besides knowledge. In A.N. Whitehead's view the justification for a university is that it preserves the connection between knowledge and zest for life, by uniting the young and the old in the imaginative consideration of learning. The University of today serves, the mass instead of few, but its duty remains that of enobling human beings. It is also said that a University is not a democracy but a republic and the professors are the aristocracy of this academic republic. They define the university by the work they do in the form of teaching, research and extension services.

A college (or a University) stands and falls by its professors. It is generally said that as the professors so is the college. They are the professors who really make or mar the image of a college. Therefore, they should carry themselves like professors with nobility, dignity and scholarship. Professors ought to be people put on perfection, bubbling with excitement over ideas. They should read, write and speak great thoughts.

Bereday asks them to "hitch their wagon to the highest stars". In essence, they need constant insistence on quality and excellence.

There are not enough competent college and University teachers to fill most of the posts that have been created to meet the demands of mass higher education. Many of them are not well qualified, but quite apart their level of performance is pulled down by the large numbers they have to teach. The working conditions are often poor and remunerations scanty. Renowned sociologist Late Edward Shils has remarked that in India, most of the teachers in institutions of higher education, teach many hours weekly for very small salaries, and many of them supplement their professional income by writing notes for students or by scrambling for examinership. They have little time or motive for improving their knowledge and their manner of teaching. Lipset, drawing on the findings of Shil's and Kleiner, however, suggests that colleges, with better trained and devoted teachers, face relatively few incidents of students' indiscipline.

Quality of the citizens depends on the quality of education and the quality of education, in its turn, depends on the quality of teachers. Therefore, with poor quality of teachers it is difficult for a nation to make significant contribution to the fund of knowlede and wisdom. It is an acknowledged fact that we have been at the receiving end of the pipe, so faor as the modern knowledge is concerned. In this age of rapid change and resultant obsolescence, unless sincere efforts are made to update the knowledge and competence of teachers, we cannot think of setting "excellence" as an aim of University education. The Education Commission (1964-66) has rightly remarked:

"A sound programme of professional education of teachers is essential for the qualitative improvement of education. Investment in teacher education can yield very rich dividends because the financial resources required are small when measured against the resulting improvement in the education of millions".

For about fifteen years enrollment in higher education grew at the rate of 13-14 per cent per year. In no country of the world did at any point of history the rate of expansion go beyond 5-6 per cent per year. Unavoidably, therefore, we paid a heavy price in dilution of standards. Nothing else was so much responsible for low standards, says Amrik Singh, as the poor quality of teachers recruited into the system. The speed of the horse-man cannot be faster than that of the horse. Hence, what the teachers imparts to their students cannot obviously be better than what they are capable of. To improve their professional competence is, therefore, a matter of paramount importance. Though, this is recognized, what is actually being done is woefully inadequate. The UGC budget funds, for quantitative expansion in the fourth plan period, were fully utilized but those meant for qualitative improvement, limited as they were, lapsed to the extent of 50 per cent. This tendency should not be allowed to continue in the subsequent plan periods including the eleventh.

Teaching is a highly skilled profession and, therefore, training should be an essential requirement for the new entrants. A lecturer in a College or University is required to take up his full load of teaching from the first day of his appointment. He starts teaching without any orientation to methods of teaching either through a formal course or through the observation of teaching of some effective teachers. He or she simply imitate the ways of teaching of his or her teacher. The new entrant designs his lectures without giving a deeper insight into the purposeful organization of his lecture. He lacks the proper understanding of needs and interests of adolescents to whom he teaches. Neither he knows the 'psychology of adolescents' nor the 'psychology of learning'. He prepares question papers and assess the answer scripts without receiving a scientific knowledge of evaluation techniques. He has no grounding to organize tutorials, seminars, discussions or workshops.

There is no tradition, in our Universities, where a junior consults his senior on professional matters. Nor is there a tradition under which a departmental head imparts, regularly, phased guidance to the new entrants in the profession. Thus, the enthusiastic recruit is left to himself and all the competencies, in course of time, are acquired by him through trial and elimination of error. If he gets through this ordeal without being wrecked, the credit goes to himself and not to the seniors or the system.

The Education Commission (1964-66) has emphasized the need for a training course for newly recruited university and college teachers. Even for the old and senior teachers programmes of continuing education are desirable in view of the exploding knowledge and techniques in the area of androgogy and education. Nearly more than one lakh journals in about 60 languages double every 6 years.

Nearly half of what a person learns is no longer valid when he reaches middle age. In the future, skills will obsolesce and facts will wear out at a more rapid rate. No one will ever 'complete' an education. Therefore, in order to arrest professional obsolescence, one must learn continuously and develop the 'knack of learning'. The National Policies on Education have, again and again reiterated the needs for professional and pedagogical preparation of college and university teachers. What John W. Gardner said, in another context, equally holds good for teaching profession: "The society which scorns excellence in plumbing because plumbing is a humble activity and tolerates shoddiness in philosophy because it is an exalted activity will have neither good plumbing nor good philosophy. Neither its pipes nor its theories will hold water". To prevent this attitude from growing further we must accept and see it implemented that "What matters most is the continuing education of the teachers" in the changing times.

Though, Academic Staff Colleges have been established for the professional preparation of college and university teachers, they have not been able to impact teaching, research and course contents of different subjects. It has been gathered by many experts in higher education that the leadership of these colleges is not in the hands of such scholar professors who have a vision and inclination for triggering a zeal for continuous professional growth in the teachers. In my opinion a rigorous academic review of the Academic Staff Colleges is needed immediately to give them feedback on their performance.

# 16

# Competency Based Teaching: Some Issues

The strength of an educational system must largely depend on the quality of its teachers. However, lofty the aims, however uptodate and abundant the equipment, however, efficient the administration; in the absence of an efficient teacher all these will prove sterile and infructuous so far as the pupils' learning is concerned. There is a growing consciousness in public and professional quarters that the 'goodness' of an educational programme depends, to a large extent, on the quality of teaching done in the classroom (Ryans, 1960). The identification of qualified and able teaching personnel, therefore, constitutes one of the most important of all educational concerns. Producing competent teachers is another obligation of education. If competent teachers can be prepared, the likelihood of attaining desirable educational outcomes is ensured to a great extent.

What is teaching? Teaching is an art, not a science.... Teaching is not like inducing a chemical reaction, it is much more like painting a picture or composing a musical melody, or on a different level like cultivating a garden or writing a personal letter. One must immerse one's heart into it, one must remember that it cannot be done by formulae or you will spoil your work and your pupils and yourself. (Highet, 1950). Teaching involves an element of spontaneous and inspiring communication between the teacher and the taughts, a form of self-expression requiring genuine creativity. The teacher in many ways resembles the prototype of an artist. The artist communicates at the same time he portrays, teaching us to see that what he portrays in the same way as he sees it. The art of talking lies similarly in the communication and projection of an essentially private experience.

There are no unquestioned or universally accepted definitions of good teaching. From times immemorial, educationists, philosophers and researchers have tried to define and explain 'good teachers'. Giving a very comprehensive definition, Jansen (1951) indicated that a good teacher is adaptable, attractive, careful, considerate, cooperative, dependable, enthusiastic, forceful, healthy, honest, industrious, neat, open-minded, original and progressive as well as informed. The gradual evolvement of this definition may be traced down the decades. The philosophic rationalists of the mid-nineteenth century put emphasis on strength of character, clarity of thinking, firmness of discipline, intelligence and scholarship (Sully, 1886). By the late ninetieth and early twentieth century, there was more talk of tough mindedness, extraversion and gift in the management of people (Welton and Balndford, 1909).

Emphasis was next put on organizing ability and on skill in the arrangement of conditions contributory to the establishment of correct habits. This was supported by a concern for clarity of analysis of the content of the curriculum, perseverence in drill and clearness in presentation (Kent, 1920). The writers of the late 1920's asked for an interest in 'citizenship'. The good teacher was one who, participating in the concerns of the community, understood the social relevance of curriculum (Mead, 1929). By the 1930's attention was turning to the significance of attitudes. A good teacher was one who showed gifts of leadership, discrimination in the assessment of seriousness of misdemeanours, along with a certain flair in the treatment of behavioural disorders, supplemented by professional skill in the use of standardized tests and the diagnosis of individual difficulties in the learning of the basic subjects (Rinsland, 1938). In the 1940's there were signs of a fuller appreciation of the adult who showed attractiveness and persuasiveness, ability to win attention as well as command support (Jackson, 1940). Recent findings by Ryans (1951) and Evans (1952) vary from ratings in open-mindedness (in the sense of the originality, adaptability and tolerance which permit participation on the part of the pupils), a business like approach in the organization of class activities, impartiality, calmness, consistency, sociability and attractiveness, intelligence and the willingness to use it in the classroom situations, to scores in objective tests of resourcefulness, social participation and interest in teaching.

Traditionally, a teacher is considered fit to teach on successful completion of certain professional and academic courses. Today, this assumption is being questioned. In its place the 'idea of competency' is gaining strength. A teacher is considered fit to teach only when she can successfully demonstrate the essential competencies required in performing the function of teaching. Traditional evaluation of teacher trainees comprises of rating the trainee's knowledge, in the theoretical course, usually represented by a grade obtained in the examinations held at the end of the course and appraisal of the trainee's teaching performance, typically represented by a grade given for practice teaching. The competency based movement calls for more detailed, fine grained evaluation of the skills, knowledge and attitudes of teacher trainees. The trainees are held responsible, not for the passing grades, but for attaining a given level of competency in performing the essential tasks of teaching.

Teaching competencies are variously defined as "... attitudes, understandings, skills and behaviours that facilitate intellectual, social, emotional and physical growth in learners" (Cooper and Weber, 1973), "... functional abilities which teachers demonstrate in the day to day job related activity" (Dodl, Norman *et al.*, 1972), "demonstrated ability to perform the functions required in a certified teaching position" (Schalock, 1973). Generally, "Teacher Competence" is the ability of a teacher to produce agreed upon educational effects. For example, a teacher's ability to modify the behaviour of pupils, when and if appropriate, is a competency. The knowledge of the principles involved like 'reinforcement' is not a competency, but the actual performance which accomplishes the end would be an evidence that the teacher possess the competence. Also, a competent teacher must demonstrate the required competency not only in the ability to perform but be able to use the ability when it is appropriate and avoid using it when it is not. Whereas competency results in reproduction of skills, performativity leads to highter order skills of imaginative reconfigurations that include competency as well as critical thinking skills to organise and evaluate information to create new knowledge.

A teacher's basic competence according to Barr (1952), imply her role as : (i) director of learning, (ii) a friend and counselor of students, (iii) a member of a group of professional workers, and (iv) a citizen participating in various community activities. Thus, we can define teacher competence as the ability to apply to practical situations, the essential principles and techniques of teaching. Reager and Partte (1973) have given importance to the following criteria for judging teacher competence: (i) knowledge of the subject to be taught, (ii) certain natural endowments such as a pleasing personality, patience, fondness for children, students' family background, social status, cognitive ability etc. Gage (1965), in a review of literature of the present time allows for the selection of five global characteristics, namely, warmth, cognitive organization, orderliness, indirectness and problem solving ability as components of effective teaching. O'Kelley (1974) indicated that an effective teacher must have a through knowledge of the subject matter, show interest in teaching students and show interest and enthusiasm for the subject. According to Yarger (1974) competent teachers would be viewed as professionals who could employ specific instructional strategies based on the objectives of the materials to be taught, the situation for teaching the characteristics of the children, and finally their own characteristics of teaching style. Haberman (1965), in his intriguing and informative study of the teaching behaviour of successful teacher trainees, identified five behavioural patterns that seemed to distinguish between successful and unsuccessful teacher trainees: (i) a behavioural demonstration of a belief in the youngsters' potentialities, (ii) an ability to organize a classroom situation, (iii) a real enthusiasm for some subject matter, (iv) an ability to set appropriate standards, and (v) a willingness to listen.

One of the major problems in education today is how to evaluate adequately the competencies required of an effective teacher. The three major obstacles reported by researchers in the area are: (i) lack of consistency regarding the precise criteria for effective teaching, (ii) consequent lack of a agreement among professional educators regarding which action patterns constitute effectiveness, and (iii) reluctance on the part of teachers to submit to intensive and prolonged investigation of their professional performances.

Another problem is what priority should be given to the many things that may be evaluated? According to McDonald (1978), the major areas of competence to be evaluated are the substantive knowledge about the content of the curricula, teaching methods, performance skills and strategies and attitudes towards teaching and learning. The logic of the argument supporting the position is that what the teacher does that directly effects how much children learn, develop and change as a consequence of being exposed to instruction. What a teacher knows about the subjects to be taught also determines what a child will learn, and teachers' attitudes will affect how they actually teach and how the children will learn.

Therefore, to assess a teacher's performance in relation to a given competency, many dimensions of the teaching learning process must be considered such as:

(i) Student population: Grade, age, class size, percentage and kinds of handicaps, level of socio-economic status, absentee rates, kinds of grouping, reading level etc.

(ii) Instructional materials: Match between curriculum purposes and materials, sufficiency of materials etc.

(iii) Curriculum: Content/subject area, degree of teacher involvement in creating curriculum etc.

(iv) Classroom setting: Light, space and furniture, black-boards, bulletin board, books shelves etc.

(v) Time allocation and utilization: Time allocated for each activity.

(vi) Distractions: Nature and kinds of interruptions, noise level etc.

(vii) Teacher: Teacher's feelings of security, ability to handle content previously taught, years of teaching, likes or dislikes of students, perceptions of their feelings etc.

Also in assessing teaching performance, certain conditions must be kept in mind like:

(i) Teaching does not occur in a vacuum, it is one component of a holistic classroom ecology.

(ii) Given a common instructional objective for the same student, it is possible that two teachers with contrasting styles could achieve similar results.

(iii) Depending upon teacher's experience, training, personalities and interests, a given teaching act or competency will be more or less difficult and this is in turn, will be affected by context variables.

As Tikunoff and Ward (1978) have very aptly pointed out: 'the act of teaching cannot be investigated successfully unless the total context of the teaching has of necessity to be carried out in naturalistic settings which allow events to occur realistically. This contention is supported by the work of Brophy (1976), Stallings (1976), McDonald (1976) and Tikunoff, Berliner and Rist (1975). Another issue that complicates the evaluation of teacher competence, is the unreliability of assessment techniques based on the observation of external behaviours of teachers. These assessment techniques tend to be reductionistic and lacking in meaning because they fail to assess the underlying causes of these behaviours of teachers. Usually the result is the assessment of behaviours which have little generalizability or transferability to a variety of teaching requirements. A trainee, for example, may acquire particular skills, but never become even a moderately effective teacher. The trainee in a microteaching programme may learn how to reinforce participation in a microclass, ask higher order questions or give clear explanations. Assessment made of skills in these particular performance tell us that the teacher trainee can enact the desired performances under a set of conditions, but they do not reveal whether the trainee can combine and integrate these skills and others into a complex strategy that can be varied from day to day and sustained over long periods of time. Managing a class, for example, occurs throughout the entire period or day, it consists of a set of skills that may be called upon for different reasons at different times. How these skills are used in day to day practice ultimately determines whether a teacher is a skillful manager.

Implicit in the behavioural objective approach is the assumption that the acquisition of micro skills and abilities add up in some linear and simplistic fashion to overall competence. Statistically speaking, specific skills may be associated with teaching success, but it does not follow that these behaviours lead to success, they may have followed it. Broudy's (1972) criticism of this supposition is useful here: "The assumption that in teaching the whole is merely the sum of parts is a notoriously inadequate description of any human action, let alone one so complex as teaching. Teaching, can of course, be thought of as broken down into parts, but as a concrete action, it is guided at every moment by a sense of judging, integrates the analyzed constituents into a meaningful functional sequence, not merely a mechanically additive one". Broudy goes on to say that how often a person has performed a specialized task or over what range, may not be as important as the ability to perform a variation of the task not previously practiced.

The implications of Broudy's comments have been summarized by Pottinger (1976): 'the preoccupation with specificity, clarity and precisions of behavioural objectives has left us with an operational paradigm, for defining and measuring teaching competencies, which is intuitively and theoretically oversimplified and invalid... Rigorous behavioural observations fail to assess adequately either complex interactions among variables or underlying causes of competent teaching performance. Too often qualities of the mind and character unamenable to direct observation techniques account for the presence or absence of competent performance.'

The alternative to the behavioural objective approach seems to be the traditional system of evaluation which is vague, abstract and unmeasurable. However, we know that competence consists of a number of complex interacting variables which are not always directly observable. Neither the knowledge of how one should teach, nor simple demonstration of the behaviour gets to the heart of competence. Links must be established between the knowledge and behaviours that constitute successful performances and their causes. Competency assessment should include factors, which cause effective use of both knowledge and behaviours in the classroom. For example, learning style is an important teacher characteristic. It would be better to define, teach, and assess the causal variables or factors that lead teachers to make such adoptions.

A holistic approach, rather than a component, competency by competency analysis of teaching, needs to be emphasized in research on teacher competence. Holistic analysis attends to the entire reality in which teaching occurs. It considers not only the quantitative occurrence of a teaching competency but also the qualitative influence upon all those involved and the implications of the competency within each particular occurrence. The stress should be laid on a combination of quantitative and qualitative methodologies in holistic analysis.

## References

Barr, A.S., Measurement of Teacher Characteristics and Prediction of Teacher Efficiency. *R. Ed. Res.,* 22: 169-174, 1952.

Brophy, J.E., Reflection on Research in Elementary Schools. *Journal of Teacher Education,* 27(1), Spring, 1976.

Broudy, H.S., A *Critique* of *Performance-Based Teacher Education:* PBTE Series No. 4, Washington D.C., American Assn. of Colleges for Teacher Education, 1972.

Cooper, J.M. and Weber, W.A., Competency Based Systems Approach to Teacher Education in Cooper, J.M. et al. (ed.), *A Systems Approach to Program Design.* Berkeley, California, McCutehan Publishing Co., 1973.

Dodl, Norman, R. *et al., The Florida Catalog* of *Teacher Competencies.* Chipley, Florida, 1972.

Evans, K.M., A Study of Teaching Ability at the Training College Stage. Ph.D. Thesis, London, 1952.

Gage, N.L., Desirable Behaviour of Teachers. *Urban Ed.,* 1 :85-95, 1965.

Haberman, M., The Teaching Behaviour of Successful Interns. *Journal of Teacher Education,* 16:215-20, June 1965.

Highet, G., *The* Art of *Teaching.* New York, Knopf, 1950.

Jackson, V.D., J. Exper. Edu. VIII. 4.422-74. 1940 in Fleming, C.M., *Teaching:* A *Psychological Analysis.* London, Methuen, 1958.

Jensen, A.C., J. Exper. Edu. XX. 1.79-85, 1951 in Fleming, C.M., *Teaching:* A *Psychological Analysis.* London, Methuen, 1958.

Kent, R.A., J. Edu. Res. II. 802-7, 1920 in Fleming, C.M., *Teaching:* A *Psychological Analysis.* London, Methuen, 1958.

McDonald, F.J., Report of Phase II of the Beginning Teacher Evaluation Study. *Journal* of *Teacher Education,* 27(1), 1976.

McDonald, F.J., Evaluating Pre-service Teachers' Competence. *Journal* of *Teacher Education,* 29(2), 1978.

Mead, A.R., J. Edu. Res. XX. 4.239-59, 1929 in Fleming, C.M., *Teaching:* A *Psychological Analysis.* London, Methuen, 1958.

O'Kelley, F.M., Student Evaluation of Teacher Effectiveness. Dissertation Abstracts International, 35:946, 1974.

Pottinger, P.S., Designing Instruments to Measure Competence. *Journal* of *Teacher Education,* 29(2), 1978.

Reager, G.M. & Pratte, R.N., An Understanding of Schools: An Aspect of Teacher Competence. *Theory into Practice,* 10: XII: 1,1973.

Rinsland, M.A., J. Exper. Edu. VI. 3.307-317, 1938 in Fleming, C.M., *Teaching:* A *Psychological Analysis.* London, Methuen, 1958.

Ryans, D.G., J. Exper. Edu. XX. 1.67-77, 1951 in Fleming, C.M., *Teaching:* A *Psychological Analysis.* London, Methuen, 1958.

Ryans, D.G., *Characteristics* of *Teacher: Their description, Comparison and appraisal.* Washington D. C., American Council on Education, 1960.

Schalock, H. D., Implications of the Oregon Board of Education's proposed "Process Standards" for the Design and Operation of Teacher Education programs: Interpretive Paper 1-Defining and Assessing Teacher Competence. Monmouth, Oregon, 1973.

Stalings, J.A., How Instructional Processes relate to Child outcomes in a National Study of Follow Through. *Journal* of *Teacher Education,* 27(1), 1976.

Sully, J., *The Teachers' Handbook* of *Psychology.* London, Longmans, 1886.

Tikunoff, W.J., Berliner, D.G. and Rist, R.C., An Ethnographic Study of Forty Classrooms of the Beginning Teacher Evaluation Study Known Sample. San Francisco, Far West Laboratory for Educational Research and Development, 1975.

Tikunoff, W.J., and Ward, Insuring Reliability and Validity in Competency Assessment. *Journal* of *Teacher Education*, 29(2), 1978.

Weldon, J. and Blandford, F.G. *Principles and Methods* of *Moral Training*. London, University Tutorial Press, 1909.

# 17

# Managing New Media in Education to Humanize Technology

The world is passing through a technetronic revolution. We, in India, are also feeling the impact of the tempo of technological change almost in every walk of life. It is a truism to say that Industry and Agriculture have made revolutions through the use of technological advancements. But the application of technology is almost at the 'dry farming' stage in the field of education in our country. We have to agree with Finn (1968) that "technology has only washed lightly on the shores of instruction".

The instructional media and teaching aids have passed through four stage. The first stage consists of pre-machine devices like charts, models, exhibits etc. The second stage includes printed or written material like text-books, reference books, work-books and teachers' notes. The third stage introduced machines like radio, linguaphone, projector, films etc.; and the fourth stage, which is coming up, depends on man-machine communication e.g., computerized instruction, online learning and language laboratories etc. Broadly speaking, the first wave of breakthrough came with the invention of paper, ink and printing, and the second wave started with the invention of photography and sound films.

Reviewing the literature on teaching devices in the *Harvard Educational Review,* Doughlas Porter (1966) has pointed out that teaching efficiency might be increased by two closely related measures:

1. the application of some demonstrably valid psychological principles derived from learning experiments, and
2. the use of teaching aids and devices.

The devices can be classified as stimulus devices, response devices and stimulus-response devices. Authors of articles on immediate reinforcer teaching devices make the following claims for their devices:

1. They are time and labour saving for teachers.
2. They are effective because they provide immediate reinforcement.
3. They are more effective in consistently delivering reinforcement than a teacher can be.
4. They can deal effectively with the range of individual differences present in a classroom.
5. They are able to teach the complex relationship involved in verbal thinking (Porter, 1966).

As the task of education increases in size and complexity, two immediate effects can be noted. Firstly, a growing demand for more highly trained professional workers, and second a tendency to marshal technological resources to assist or amplify the efforts of professional workers to reduce the drain of mechanical and repetitive chores on them. Both quantitatively and qualitatively we have here a truly formidable task. Never before has any society been faced with the problem of providing so much learning to so many and with so much at stake. Never before has any society had a greater potential to train the necessary teaching force and provide teachers with such powerful tools to do their work. This is one of the greatest challenges of our time (Brown, 1965).

Modern teaching calls for integrated and highly organized use of instructional resources. But, the present educational scene is dominated by the persistence of traditional patterns of instructional organization and practice on the one hand and the encroachment of new idea and new technology on the other. For this reason, our uses of educational media are still uncertain and experimental, and administrative provisions for their management are tenuous, varied and changing, to say the least.

Making systematic use of the various educational media seems to suggest some examination of the total range of technological resources, and explorations of the need for coordination. Whether this would be desirable in any particular case may depend not only upon such general considerations as coordination and economy, but also upon the circumstances of the local situation, the size of the institution, the existing physical facilities, the personalities involved, and that alwayst depends upon a delicate balance of the traditional past and the emerging shape of the future. However, it is assumed that at some level of administrative planning and organization, all facets of the instructional-communications technology must be viewed as parts of a comprehensive whole.

Some questions generally asked are: Why not leave educational technology to the technicians? Why must professionally trained persons be used for this work? One answer to these questions has been given quite pointedly by Charles F. Hoban, Jr. (1962), Professor of Communication at the University of Pennsylvania:

"The problem of new media in education, as with almost all of the problems of new technologies, are not those of mechanics or the machinery involved. The engineers and technicians do a reasonably good job with the mechanics and the machinery of technology. The real difficulty is much more complex. It arises from the reorganization of procedures, the introduction and wider use of management on a higher level of skill, the changing role of the men and women in the process of system, and the evaluation of goals made possible by the productivity of technology". Dr. Shib K. Mitra (1977) also endorses this viewpoint and stresses the need of organizational skill and management of a high order to utilize educational technology in a fruitful manner.

The problem will be solved neither by employing more administrative personnel nor by simply buying more films, more books or more projectors. We, in fact, need an insightful recognition of the proper roles of instructional media services as required by changes in curriculum goals and patterns, the nature and size of our student group, and the teacher classroom needs.

The long-delayed advance of technology in education has entered a stage of acceleration. Increasing use of newer media in the classroom in the organization and scheduling of classes. Sometimes, rather drastic changes in instructional procedures, striking at the very heart of the teacher-pupil relationship, are required. Many teachers feel threatened because they believe that the technological advances tend to generate greater distance between the teacher and the taught. Shimabukuro (1964) points out that the earlier audio-visual media, including films, filmstrips, slides, recordings, display and three dimensional materials, were not so threatening because they did not disturb the central role of the teacher in the instructional dialogue. With the new instructional media, designed to teach the core of various courses, the teacher is robbed of his star role and is reduced to the ignominy of an aide.

With the growing use of technology in classroom teaching, people have started asking many questions. Will this tend to "dehumanize" the instructional process? Will instructional technology displace or degrade the teacher? Will it place too much emphasis upon efficiency and economy, and too little upon quality? Will it tend to overcentralize curriculum control and weaken the social autonomy in education? These questions are real. But, the answer is not the negation of technology or refusing its benefits but facing its dangers and taming it in such a way that it does not deprive us of our humanity. A humanized technology can, on the contrary, free the teacher from the servitude of mechanical and routine chores and amplify the force of his creative and distinctively human efforts. The aim is to help people assert more powerful, more creative and more humane roles in teaching through technology. When Mumford and Maslow talk about "humanizing" the machine, they are, perhaps, talking about humanizing people. This can be done by bringing up the use of educational technology (or machine) under the control of purpose that are informed and truly humane.

## References


Brown, James W., *Administering Educational Media.* New York, McGraw-Hili Book Company, 1965.

Finn, J.D. and Perrin, D.G., Teaching Machines and Programmed Learning. In Shaw, G. B. *et al.*, *Technology Knocks at the door of Education.* Baroda: Centre of Advance Study in Education, 1970.

Hoban, Charles, F., The New Media and the School. *Audio- Visual Communication Review,* November-December 1962, 10, 354.

Lumsdaine, A.A. and Glaser Robert (Ed.), *Teaching Machines and Programmed Learning: A Source Book,* Washington: National Education Association, 1966.

Mitra, Shib, K., New Direction in Education. *IAPL & EI Journal,* January 1977,1(1), 13-23.

Porter, Douglas, A Critical Review of a Portion of the Literature on Teaching Devices. In Lumsdaine, A.A. et al. (Eds.), *Teaching Machines and Programmed Learning:* A *Source Book,* Washington: National Education Association, 1966.

Shimabukuro, Shinkichi, Programmed Instruction: Threat or Challenge? *Audio-visual Instruction,* May 1964, 9, 277.

# 18

# Instructional Strategies for Improved Learning from Distance Teaching Materials

Distance education is a strand of non-formal education. It takes place in the absence of teacher-taught interface. Being controlled and regulated from a distance, it is also called "remote controlled" or "tele-communication" education. The physical separation of teacher and learner envisages a different role for the teacher. He may meet the students only for "selected tasks' such as counseling, giving tutorials or seminars or solving study problems.

## Effect of Media

The growing awareness that learning, not teaching is the decisive factor in education has brought support to distance education along with other methods of independent study (Holmberg 1980). Distance education is often distinguished from 'correspondence study' by the notion of three way-teaching. It can be equated with the combined, systematic and flexible use of at least three major elements: print-based communication, broadcasting (and/or other technologies), and face-to-face contact in support of an independent learner (Kaye, 1985). Out of these elements, face to face communication is transacted for a very short duration.

So far as the effects of media of mass communication are concerned, five decades of research (in U.S.A.) suggest that there are no learning benefits to be gained from employing different media in instruction, regardless of their obviously attractive features or advertised superiority (Clark, 1983). "The best current evidence is that media are mere vehicles that deliver instruction but do not influence student achievement any more than the truck that delivers our groceries causes change in our nutrition. Basically, the choice of vehicle might influence the cost or extent of distributing instruction, but only the content of vehicle can influence achievement." While research often shows a slight learning advantage for newer media over more conventional instructional vehicles, this advantage will be shown to be vulnerable to compelling rival hypothesis. It is the uncontrolled effects of novelty and instructional method which account for the existing evidence for the effects of various media on learning. Therefore the text material still remains a powerful and popular mode of presenting and transmitting large amount of knowledge in a well organized and psychologized way to the learners (Chaudhari. 1986).

**Power of Print Media:**

"By far the most important medium in distance education" says Holmberg (1981) "is the printed word. This applies to conventional correspondence study as well as to highly sophisticated multi-media presentation like courses of the Open University". Although the choice of media depends on the nature of subject matter, print media has been found largely effective in each of the cognitive, affective and psychomotor domain. Zuber (1981) of the University of South Pacific also pleads that "any medium-can generally be regarded to a greater or lesser degree as support for course material in form of print. Care must always be taken that this existing and fundamental medium should not be overlooked. Researches done in the area of 'learning from text' (Anderson 1972-73: Frase, 1970: Mayer, 1977: Rothkopf, 1965) reveal that the written word is more effective in certain domains than the other. If the objective is cognitive, involving analysis as in philosophy, the printed work will probably be more effective (Nashif, 1981).

**Cognitive Emphases for Better Learning**

Cognitive psychologists and educators have designed certain instructional strategies to help teachers convey large amount of information as meaningfully and efficiently as possible in the conventional formal groups situations as well as in "learning at home" individual setting.

Though, there is considerable variation in opinions as to how one can use cognitive learning research and theory in the formulation of instructional principles, yet some characteristic emphases can be discerned:

1. Cognitive learning theorists emphasize the importance of cognitive process in the planning of instruction.
2. They propose that the student should be conceptualized as a processor of information, who actively selects and interprets certain stimuli from all those which impinge on him, in he learning situation.
3. The major task of the instructor is to provide whatever guidance seems necessary to help the learner to organize new information in a meaningful way. There is a distinct preference for featuring situations which stimulates inquiry search patterns, and for avoiding those situations which make the student a passive recipient of facts to be memorized by rote practices.
4. It is expected that guides will be given as to how the learner might structure the information either through 'advance organizers' or through other features provided by the teacher or the educational materials.

5. In designing their instructional procedures, cognitive theorists draw as extensively form psychology's developmental theory as they do from learning theory. Though the emphasis is more in age group patterns than on individual difference, yet they seem to be as aware as any other instructional theorist about the need for considering individual differences in planning instruction.
6. Cognitive theorists seem to divide their concerns for improving educational practice equally between curricular reforms and instructional method innovations. They emphasize that the structure must be meaningful for the learner, no matter whether it is meaningful for professional educations. It is also held that more active, exploratory, discovery learning procedures will assist the learners in organizing new information and integrating it with his existing knowledge.
7. In the instructional materials or in the directions provided by the teacher, there should be some means whereby the student can develop skills in evaluating his own progress (Snelbacker, 1974).

Learning is an ongoing life activity and not one confined to studying for examinations. Without knowing how we learn individuals are not realizing their full potentials (Elliot and Wright, 1980); Pace (1985) states that learners can be thought to analyse learning tasks and generate questions to test their understanding. She recommends that any instructional material designed to improve 'learning to learn' should explicitly describe the main points of the learning, how they are related and how they might be interrelated with what the learner already knows. If such methods of study and recall are to be helpful to the learner in the process of learning to learn, devices such as 'advance organizers', 'interspersed questions' and 'tutorial letters' should be used.

**Advance organizer**

'Advance organizer' is a derivative of the Meaningful Verbal Learning Theory advanced by David P. Ausubel. The learner consciously acts upon the concept or proposition in an attempt to remember it so that is will be available at some future time. He may attempt to retain the idea by relating it, substantively and non-arbitrarily, to what he knows, and thereby make sense out of it, then meaningful learning will result.

Ausubel defined 'advance organizers' as introductory material (or super ordinate statement) at a higher level of abstraction, generality and inclusiveness than the learning passage itself. They are not a summary presentations of the principal ideas in a passage. Advance organizers also differ from 'overviews' in being relatable to presumed ideational content in the learners' current cognitive structure (Ausubel, 1978). In brief, an 'advance organizer' is a 'cognitive bridge' between the existing perceptual data of the learner and the new to-be-learned material. It also acts as an 'intellectual scaffolding', or 'ideational anchorage' for the learners to fit in and structure the ideas and facts they encounter in the learning material which follows the principle of progressive differentiation and integrative reconciliation in its organization of presentation.

Ausubbl (1968) theory of meaningful verbal learning states that there is a parallel between the way subject matter is organized in a discipline and the way people organize knowledge in their mind or cognitive structure. The concepts, in a discipline and in a person's cognitive structure, are arranged in hierarchies. For meaningful incorporation of new material into cognitive structure, general, relevant concepts called 'subsumers' must exit to which the new concepts can be linked. When appropriate subsumers either do not exist or are unclear and unstable, rote learning occurs. Ausubel further suggested using an advance organizer to provide a subsumer when none exists or to make more clear and stable a pre-existing one.

The advance organizers facilitate learning and retention in three ways. First, if properly designed, they call attention to and build on those relevant anchoring ideas which the learner already has in his cognitive structure. For example, the advance organizer would refer to fundamental concepts and principles learned in previous lessons and would relate them to the material which is to be learned. Second, they provide a kind of scaffolding for the new material by encompassing the areas to be covered and by delineating the fundamental ideas under which the rest of the information can be subsumed. Third, the kind of stable and clear organization essentially renders unnecessary having the learner learn the material by rote memorization. Ausubel contends that avoidance of rote learning procedures will have a positive motivating influence on the students and will actually make the newly learned information far more useful in subsequent real-life situations (Snelbacker, 1974).

Facilitative effect of advance organizes have been confirmed by a large number of studies (Chaudhari, 1981 and 1985-86; Doyle, 1986; Mayer, 1979). Kozlow (1978) and Luiten *et al.* (1980) made a meta analysis of studies conducted from 1960 to 1980. In all the 135 studies analysed by Luiten *et al.*, the most important feature considered was the magnitude of the effect of advance organizers on learning and retention. The analysis of influence of grade level on learning and retention revealed that 'college level' was the most beneficiary in terms of learning, and primary level did better in retention. Thus, by and large, the findings indicate that advance organizers facilitate learning in almost all content areas and with individuals of all grade and ability levels.

## Interspersed Questions

Questions are a major force in shaping the nature of student' thought and methods of inquiry because they act as motivational stimuli and have arousal and associative.

outcomes. Anderson (1967) states that a question is a critical variable for controlling learning behaviours. According to him the most compelling stimulus in a frame is the questions which must be answered or the blank must be completed. A basic problem involved in the effective control of learning behaviour notes Frase (1968), thus may not be whether the material is broken in to small steps or physically separated in stimulus and responses terms, but whether the method of instructional control (be it a programme frame, a question or a graph) gets the student to practice the stimuli and responses, and to make the appropriate associations between the two.

Summarizing researches on learning from written materials Frase (1970) stated three characteristics of questions influencing learning: (a) their position in text, (b) the contiguity of questions and related content, and (c) the type of question. In general it was found that subjects learn most when the questions come after the material to which they relate. Studies have shown that questioned groups, in comparison to a control group, which did not see adjunct questions, retained more of the questions related material. Post-question groups retained somewhat more incidental information than the pre-question groups. The post-questions work best when the motivation is low and they occur after small amounts of text.

There were no differences in retention between pre and post-question groups when the questions occurred every 50 sentences. But, when questions occurred after every 10 sentences, the post-question groups scored about 40% higher on over all retention than the pre-question groups. Therefore, contiguity of the questions and their related content might work either for or against overall retention depending upon the point at which the reader views a question, i.e., immediately before or after he reads the text.

There is little doubt that the type of question posed is an important determinant of the behaviours that the reader/ learner will exhibit. For instance, Rothkopt and Bisbicos (1967) interspersed in a text those questions related to either common or technical terms. Their design involved pre- and post-question groups. The post-question groups that had seen technical term questions showed high recall of other technical terms. Frase (1968) explored the effects of pre-questions that vary in the amount of material to which they related. Subjects were asked to underline the amount of information in a text which would be required to answer a specific pre-question, a comparative question, or a general question. The subjects' responses indicated that the number of words perceived to be necessary to answer the questions increased in the order of specific, comparative and then general questions.

Distance learning study guides very often contain questions in the text. These may be short or long and may be self evaluating or require assignments to be submitted. Whichever of these options is used, the main point is that the questions are inserted in order to involve the student actively and guide him as to the pace at which progress is being made (Yule, 1985).

The types of questions may also vary from a low level such as those only requiring a yes/no or true/false response to a high level requiring a well-reasoned lengthy answer. Obviously, the latter could not be self-assessed and thus in the study guide the more commonly used questions are of a low order requiring a response that can be marked by referring back to the text. "All things considered, it would appear that a useful rule-of-thumb for writers would be to insert a high-level question after each section of text material dealing with an important theme, topic, issue, theory or similar substantive unit" (Marland and Store, 1982).

**Letters as Pedagogical Device in Distance Education**

Six investigations carried out at the university of South Africa have revealed that students regard the tutorial letters as 'irreplaceable' in the study package (Van As, 1983). During the course of a year the tutorial letters that are sent out maintain a link between teacher and student and form a vital part of the interactive feedback system in distance learning. A tutorial letter has also been found helpful in pacing the students who are learning at home. Presently, tutorial letters written to students stationed in remote areas contain vital information for assignments and guidelines for studying a particular course. They are hardly being used to transmit fundamental knowledge.

The potential of "letter form" of communication has not been exploited for pedagogical/anthropological purposes in our country. Letters written from jail by Jawaharlal Nehru to his daughter Indira Gandhi amply illustrates the pedagogical power and potential of 'letters' for distance education.

A letter is a personal and persuasive form of communication, and therefore it can be used on the one hand to motivate, to provide on 'advance organizer' and to reduce academic isolation of the distant learner; and on the other to transmit knowledge in a lively or "talk to" style from a distance. It has been found by E. Paul Torrance in his studies on creative reading that the use of personal pronoun like "I" in thc text material increased the involvement of the reader and thereby raised his achievement. If the language used in the materials employs a personal style which "talk to" the learner, he will find the materials interesting and worth studying.

Thus, we have seen that the logical structure of the written material and provision of opportunity for search in it contribute to thc improvement of learning. Adroitly presented, 'orienting directions' also play an important role in disposing the reader to respond to certain aspects of text. General instructions to learn, advance organizers, various cuing strategies, questions and tutorial letters are some of the important classes of orienting directions. In order to make distance learning more effective these strategies and 'aids to study' should be integrated in to the learning material and study guides.

**References**

Anderson, R.C. Learning concepts from definitions *American Educational Research Journal*, 1972, 9, 385-390.

Anderson, R.C. Learning Principles form text. *Journal of Educational Psychology*, 1973, 26-30.

Anderson, R.C. & Faust, G.W. The effects of strong formal prompts in programmed instruction. *American Educational Research Journal*, 1967, 4, 345-352.

Ausubel, D.P. In defense of advance organizers: A reply to critics. *Review of Educational Research*, Spring 1978, 48, 251-257.

Ausuble, D.P. *The Psychology of Meaningful Verbal Learning* New York: Grune and Stratton, 1963.

Chaudhari, U.S. *Issues and advances in education*. Delhi; Ajanta Book International, 1986.

Chaudhari, U.S. Effects of advance organizers on learning from text in relation to sex and socio-economic status. *Journal of Education and Psycholgy*, Octo. 1985 & Jan. 1986, 43, 158-163.

Chaudhari, U.S. Educational technology research: Whole Vs. Part Presentation of Advance Organizers in Text in relation to Intelligence. *Educational Technology (U.S.A.)*, June 1981, 32-35.

Clark, Richard E. Reconsidering research on learning from media. *Review of Educational Research.* Winter 1983, 53, 445-459.

Doyle, William H. Using the advance organizer to establish a subsuming function concept for facilitating achievement in remedial college mathematics. *American Educational Research Journal*. Full 1986, 23, 507-516.

Elliot, K. and Wright D. *Skills of the eighties: Learning skill programme*, Available from 22 Burrell Close. Prenton, Birkenhead. Merseside L 428 QE.

Frase, L.T. Boundary conditions for Mathemagenic behaviours. *Review of Educational Research*, June, 1970, 40, 337-347.

Frase, L.T. Questions as aids to reading: Some research and theory. *American Educational Research Journal*, 1968, 5, 319-332.

Frase, Lawrence T. Structure and learning from written materials. In Arthur M. Taylor (Chm.), *Educational implications of research on elaboration, imagery and memory*, Symposium presented at the annual meeting of the American Educational Research Association. Mnneapolis, March, 1970.

Holmberg, B. Distance study at post graduate level, working document presented to Symposium on Distance Education for the updating of knowledge at Post Graduate level, Unesco, Madrid, 1980.

Holmberg, B. *Status and trends in distance education*, London; Kogam Page, 1981.

Kays, A.R. Distance Education. In Torsten Husen *et a1.* (ed), *The International Encyclopedia of Education*. Oxford: Pergamon Press, 1985.

Kozlow, M.J. A meta-analysis of selected advance organizer research reports from 1960-1977 (Doctoral Dissertation, The Ohio State University, 1978). *Dissertation Abstract International*, 1978, 39, 5047 B.

Luiten, J. Ames, W. and Ackerson, G.A meta-analysis of the effect of advance organizers on learning and retention. *American Educational Research Journal*. 1980, 17, 211-218.

Marland, P.W. and Store, R.E. Some instructional strategies for improved learning from distance teaching materials. *Distance Education*, 1982, 3, 72-103.

Mayer, Richard E. The sequencing of instruction and the concept of assimilation-to-schema. *Instructional Science*, 1977, 6, 369-388.

Mayer, Richard E. Can advance organizers influence meaningful learning? *Review of Educational Research* 1979, 49, 371-383.

Nashif, A.M. Communication media - An integral part of a distance education curriculum. Paper presented to RSDTA. Penang (Malaysia), 1981.

Pace A..J. Learning to learn through text design: can it be done? In Jonassen, D.H. (ed.). *The Technology of Text: Principles of structuring, designing and displaying text.* Engle-wood cliffs, New Jersey: Educational Technology Publications, 1985.

Rothopf, E.Z. Some theoretical and experimental approaches to problems in written instruction, In J.D. Krumboltz (ed.). *Learning and the educational process*. Chicago: Rand McNully, 1965.

Rothkopf, E.Z. and Bisbicos, E.E. Selective facilitative effects of interspersed questions on learning from written materials. *Journal of Educational Psychology*, 1967, 58, 56-61.

Snelbecker, Glenn E, *Learning theory, instructional theory, and psychological design*. New York: McGraw Hill Book Company, 1974.

Van As, B.S. Results of investigations into study strategies. *Progression*, 1983, 5, 5-75 (In Yule, 1985).

Yule, Ronald M. The problem of pacing a student learning at home. *PLET* (Programmed Learning and Educational Technology), November 1985, 22, 315-319.

Zuber, Charles, The University of the South Pacific's experience in the use of media for distance education. Paper presented to RSDT A, Penang (Malaysia).

# 19

# Privatization and Commercialization of Higher Education

Following declaration of the New Economic Policy in 1990-91, major changes were introduced in the Indian economy under the aegis of the International Monetary Fund and the World Bank. They have made an adverse impact on higher education. The three major policy options suggested by the World Bank in 1986 for developing countries are being implemented now in our country. This policy include three components:

1. Recovering the public cost of higher education and reallocating government spending towards the level that produces the highest social returns;
2. Developing a credit market for education, together with selective scholarships, especially for higher education; and
3. Decentralizing the management of public education and encouraging institutions supported by the community and the private sector.

It is felt that these policy measures can only benefit the privileged and well-to-do sections of the society as the entire mechanism of admissions is now based on the market forces.

These changes or reforms will either make or break educational policy in India in the next decade (Shotton, 1998).

As a result of these economic measures the government started withdrawing financial support to the universities and colleges. The institutions of higher learning were asked to generate their own funds for creating infrastructure facility and to meet the running cost of higher education. Privatization was also encouraged by the center and the state governments. To meet the challenge of 'resource crunch', number of self-financed vocational and technical courses were started in the universities and colleges. Exorbitantly high fee is charged from the students of these courses making them unaccessible to the deserving poor students. This crisis situation prompted the administration of the universities and colleges to have link or partnership with the industry and business. Consultancy, community cooperation, fieldwork, applied research, and alumni support were some other crutches which were sought and employed to liberate higher education from financial mayhem.

## Colonization and corporatization of universities

In the knowledge-driven society and economy, on the one hand, it is expected that the universities and colleges should act as laboratories for producing new ideas and innovative practices, while on the other, they are being deprived of financial assistance from the governmental agencies. Tony Blair (1999) in one of his recent lecture in the Oxford University emphasized that for the competitive survival of the UK in the knowledge economy, entrepreneurial universities are as much important as entrepreneurial business. The universities should, therefore, do much more to foster a new entrepreneurial spirit and drive. But in UK also universities were compelled to close some of the teaching departments for want of funds. They had to redesign programmes to attract students from other countries and to bend themselves to become intellectual coolies of business and industries.

The frustrating outcome of governments' withdrawal of financial support, in the words of Baldwin (1994), is that "university culture is being colonized by the interrelated cultures of business, industry, and advertising...... The concept of colonization implies something much more far reaching and fundamental than the imposition of a different culture's definition, perception and constructions of meaning". Similarly, analyzing the impact of globalization on the concept of modern university, Peters and Roberts (1999) have sounded a caution that "the language of managerialism with a focus on strategic planning, mission statements, and performance indicators seems to have nothing to do with the traditional governance of the university, and the further the university moves away from the old structure the more it loses its institutional uniqueness and looks like just another corporation".

**Higher Education and WTO's Marketplace Orientation**

In these days of globalization world- affairs are conducted according to the hegemonic goodwill or hierarchy of economic interests of the first world. Higher education is increasingly seen as a commercial product to be bought and sold like any other commodity. Commercialization of higher education has reached now the global marketplace. The World Trade Organization (WTO) is considering a series of proposals to include higher education as one of its concerns, ensuring that the import and export of higher education be subject to complex rules and legal arrangements of the WTO protocols and free of restrictions (Altbach, 2001). It is feared that growing commercialization of higher education is a threat to the concept and core functions of higher education. The WTO's marketplace orientation and initiatives will destroy one of the greatest social inventions known as 'university'.

The universities have been established in the developing countries to meet their specialized academic aspirations, to contribute to national development and to modernization of the society. This social mission of the university will be greatly hampered by the WTO's philosophy of 'market fundamentalism'. The complexion of the academic institutions will be altered and the universities will be emaciated beyond recognition by the pressures of marketplace. As soon as the universities are captured by the culture of capitalism, they will get reduced to the level of corporations like Enron and Tyco noted for their fraudulent practices and unethical accounting.

**Mediocritization of Higher Education**

Excepting a few, most of the institutions of higher education in our country are not maintaining the standard and the quality necessary for surviving in the competitive world. We are lagging behind the advance countries in terms of adequacy, dynamism and international comparability of the standards. The nation is at risk on account of the rising tide of mediocrity in the institutions of higher learning. Mediocritization is visible in teaching, research and extension work. The capacity of the product of higher education to solve the basic problems of the masses has been questioned a number of times. The question of relevance of higher education, in its present form and content, for the Indian society has also been raised in many studies and reports of the committees. No doubt, the system of higher education in our country is crisis-ridden and its collapse is imminent, yet nothing substantial is being done to stem the rot. J.D. Sethi (1987) has raised a pertinent question: "Is it the collapse of the social conscience or just of a sub-system ?" To him what seems crystal clear is that "as against the promise of education exercising a liberating influence and declassing those entering the university, it has produced a highly irresponsible super elite who have cradled at the top a distinctive style of popular bigotry." The process of privatization and commercialization will further deteriorate the situation and hasten the collapse of higher education.

**March for Money and Blunting of Conscience**

It has been observed that till 90s higher education was inflicted by nepotism, sycophancy, casteism and authoritarianism. With the advent of new economic policy in the year 1990-91 the slogan of 'resource crunch' started resounding in the precincts of the universities and the colleges. Financial assistance and grants were curtailed for the purpose of stability and structural adjustment programmes. Gradually the union and the state governments began to withdraw their financial support and asked the institutions of higher learning to generate their own funds and resources. Simultaneously, privatization of higher education, was encouraged. Thus money entered the scene and started playing its part as it was doing elsewhere. Along with money the habits, attitudes and values associated with commerce and trade got imported in to the 'kingdom of knowledge' and the 'life of mind'. 'Human smithy' was endangered by 'gold smithy' and the march for money slowed down the pace for scholarship. After almost seventeen years, since the day the new economic policy began casting its shadow on higher education, we found great deterioration in the academic values and professional commitment of the teachers and educational administrators. Growing materialization in the universities and anti-intellectualism in the teaching profession have blunted the 'dissenting conscience' and dimmed the 'creative brilliance' of the teachers and the students. Even professors and scientists of universities have been found using research facilities and equipments for the benefit of companies and industries to raise money for themselves.

The society is becoming market-centric day by day. Social institutions and organizations are also being influenced by this phenomenon. Educational institutions cannot remain insulated from the market mechanism. Student's choices of careers and preferences for courses and management of the educational institutions are guided and driven by the needs of the market.

In the last 10-15 years, an unprecedented increase in the number of students in the courses of studies like commerce, economics and management has been witnessed. Institutions purveying these courses are proliferating. There is a great concern among the parents and the students for the acquisition of marketable knowledge. Computer science and software engineering courses are also getting popular with young students because of the impressive presence of the Indian software companies in the Silicon Valley in the USA, and the great demand of software specialists in Germany, UK and Japan. The academic world regulated by the dynamics of demand and supply, has acquired the essential character of the market. People are getting worldly wise and swamped in the short-term gains. The ultimate objective of intimacy with truth, beauty, wisdom and nobility is viewed with skepticism and as an 'epistemological deception'. Those who uncritically conform to the forces of market and worship it like god, have perhaps no time to listen to the noble laureate Saul Bellow, who informs us that for him the "university has been a place of divestiture where he is able to find help in the laborious task of discarding bad thoughts". If we don't take notice of such valuable words, we are surely heading towards an academic harakiri.

**Commoditization of Man and Nature**

Studying the 'Delusion of Progress' Will Durant observed that "trade made cities, cities made universities, universities made science, science made industry and industry made progress'. Once every industry was an art, now every art is an industry". With the institutionalization of the market, man has been reduced to 'man-hour' and a craft-man to a 'hand'. A visionary scholar Karl Polyani, in his classic work: *The Great Transformation,* has portrayed how captalism and its siblings succeeded in turning the bounty of nature and people's work energy or creativity into commodities. Thus the art of healing has become a commercial industry, education a matter of degrees that can be bought and clean air and water carry a price tag. In Polyani's opinion the central flaw of market fundamentalism is that: "Instead of the economy being embedded in social relations, social relations are embedded in the economic system". Since the current model of market mechanism is based on individual self-interest, it tends to disregard cooperation and altruism. According to George Soros, an authority on capitalism, the world capital markets function in an amoral fashion. The system of markets is a 'supply-demand-price' syndrome. Free market determines only price but not values and ideas. If the rules and rituals of market are allowed to govern the rest of social and economic life, particularly education, health and religion, then civilization and culture are bound to be debased and endangered (In Bakshi, 2000).

**Self-finance courses and Mercenarization of Teachers**

The tradition of private education was there in the country before the advent of British rule, but it was strictly and strongly guided by the sense of social responsibility without a grain of profit - motive or money minting. Education then was not a commercial proposition. Today almost 75% of colleges for general education and over 50% of colleges for professional education are privately managed. Based on an intensive study of 7 colleges in Kanpur, Nirmal Singh (1983) has examined the nature and consequences of the resulting 'seize' of public education by private control. His analysis reveals that with the emergence of second and successive generations of private managements, the early munificence and genuine concern for education have waned. With the increasing possibility of converting educational resources into non-educational services and goods, the private management came to acquire more and more the characteristics of a specialized 'pure' management. The perspectives in respect of the Kanpur Colleges displayed by Nirmal Singh's analysis may well be true for private colleges elsewhere in the country.

The management of self-financed courses started in the universities and colleges to over come the financial constraints tell almost the same story of misuse of funds, autocratic attitude of the head of the department and mercenarization of teachers. As these courses were started in a great haste without availability of infrastructure and qualified teachers, sanctity and quality of education have gone down. The exorbitant amount of fees charged for various vocation-oriented courses have almost displaced the learners from poverty-stricken homes out of the new academic scene. Laxity granted to the various departments and colleges to generate their own funds has resulted into unaccountability and chaos so far as the financial management is concerned. In this situation the so-called visiting faculties are flourishing and the students are suffering and languishing in their academic pursuits. The regular courses have been deprived of the inputs made available by the UGC and the state governments as these are being used by the students studying in the self-financed courses. Teachers are seen more interested in teaching the students of these courses than those of the regular ones, because of the additional monetary benefits. Visiting teachers come to teach with non-serious and casual attitudes. Easy money or remuneration without accountability, disbursed by the authorities of the self-financed courses has reduced education to a ritual without faith and commitment. The atmosphere of the university and college teaching department has been polluted. The race for excellence has been replaced by the lust for money leading to the corruption of conscience of the teachers and the administrators.

## Myths and Reality of Privatization and Vulgar Commercialization

J.B.G. Tilak (1993) has examined some myths and facts about privatization of higher education on international plane. In fact, besides political and ideological debates, privatization of higher education has been challenged on the basis of hard-core empirical evidences. Tilak exploded 'eight myths' about privatization of higher education by collecting and using empirical facts and evidences. These myths relate to the claim of superiority of private higher education in terms of input; output, quality, internal efficiency, employment, rate of social return, research, profit-motive, clientele, equality and politicization. The grand myth of overall superiority of private higher education has been demolished by Tilak with the help of data and evidences collected from developed and developing countries. Management of private colleges and universities is mostly driven by profit motives. As a result, private higher education has become almost synonymous with 'vulgar commercialization'. It mostly caters to the needs of the privileged or elite class. In most countries, the private higher education institutes offer low capital- intensive courses of study. They are also involved in providing cheap commercial and vocational studies.

The private sector has also entered into professional areas and started medical and engineering colleges for quick and huge profits. Research and broad educational needs of the society are rarely met by the private institutions. Quality and efficiency of private sector higher education is largely very poor. Therefore public universities are preferred to private ones by a large number of students for educational and financial reasons. In point of fact, private institutions are not totally private, at least from a financial standpoint. Private higher education in our country is accentuating social and economic disparities by overlooking the needs of meritorious students coming from poverty ridden families. The State or public sector is not prepared and equipped to counteract the market forces. The disadvantaged youth aspiring for higher education is feeling frustrated and getting angry with the managers of private and public sectors for displaying an unprotective and indifferent attitude.

Commercial activities are normal and essential in any civil society. A free market is governed and guided by the imperatives of demand, supply and price. In this business like approach maximization of profit is not considered unethical. Although, nowadays, the concept of 'ethical trade' and commerce is gaining ground, yet it will take a long time for ethics to influence market and business. Unlike business, education is a 'moral enterprize' and it has much to do with social justice and equality of opportunity for those who are culturally deprived and wish to access the facilities of higher education. It is therefore thought unethical to raise the fees and cost of higher education beyond a reasonable limit.

If education is allowed to be subservient to the mechanism and practices of business, it would be almost impossible for the deserving students from depressed and disadvantaged families to enter into the institution of higher learning. It is, therefore, the moral obligation of the government of a welfare state to come forward to extend financial support to the needy and deserving students in the form of freeships, scholarship, fellowship and easy loan facility.

## Rehabilitation of Disastered Higher Education

The size and diversity of our country dictates that we should try to strike a balance between public and private sectors to provide quality and reasonably priced higher education to all deserving aspirants. The key factor which compelled the government to withdraw from its role in higher education is non-availability of funds to support and subsidize. Granting autonomous status to almost all the colleges, without examining their past performance and credibility and to ask them to raise their own resources is a bad strategy to get over financial crisis. Even in the present situation the state and the central government can do much to strengthen the public sector in higher education, provided they have got the political will. There are alternative methods through which the government can motivate the well to do section of the society, particularly business and industry houses, alumni and NRIs to liberally contribute towards a 'National Endowment Fund for Higher Education'. Crisis and collapse of higher education is a bigger disaster than earthquake, flood or cyclone. Earthquakes ruin the lives and property of a few thousands, but breakdown of the higher education system may atrophy future generations and paralyze national development. Renowned historian H.G. Wells has perhaps, correctly estimated the value of education by saying: "Human history is a race between education and catastrophe". If we really bother for the betterment of human race then we ought to do everything possible on our part to enable education to win the race.

So far, a number of measures have been suggested by various agencies and experts to meet the challenges of escalating cost and financial destitution of higher education. Some of them are: upward revision of the tuition fees, education-loan, graduate tax (paying for education from future earnings), employer or user tax, education cess or levy and, above all, economy, austerity and optimum utilization of available resources. Technology can also be employed to reduce the cost of education and to make learning effective and interesting. Online learning or e-Iearning can be given some space in the formal institutions of education. The UNESCO Commission on Education for the 21st Century (1996) chaired by Jacques Delors, has made an important recommendation in this regard. It is desired by the commission that the debts be swapped for educational programmes. Education, being a long-term economic, social and human investment, too often gets sacrificed in adjustment plans. An effort must, therefore, be made to offset the adverse effects on education budgets of adjustments policies and policies for the reduction of domestic and foreign deficits. To swap debt for education, "A country's foreign debt is bought, discounted, in hard currency by a development agency (usually an international non-governmental organization) from the commercial banks or other creditors. It is then partly redeemed by the debtor country in local currency through its central bank and this amount in local currency is then used exclusively for financing (sometimes over quite long periods) particular education programmes." Since the main creditors are governments and official multilateral credit agencies, the commission feels that they should investigate the possibility of taking part themselves in swap agreement of this kind, and in devising new schemes for linking debt-relief to long-term increases in social spending.

**Regulation and Change in Behavior of Management**

Lethargy of the state and the short-term perspective of most private initiatives in higher education are responsible for the failure to create a serious rival to public institutions. Private institutions of higher education, in general, are not sound academic and financial projects, but rather short-term profit making attempts. This is confirmed by the type of courses offered, fast expansion, absence of research activities, moon-lighting of the staff of public institutions for teaching, politicking and lack of enthusiasm toward quality assessments issues. If it has provided a good business to some, it has compromised the future credibility of an important component of the system. If the development of a true competitive system is to be attained, then it is necessary that the managers of most private institutions change the behaviour that they have demonstrated so far.

The recent experience of privatization of higher education in different countries shows that the introduction of market mechanisms is a complex learning process that can not be expected to produce effective regulations instantly, and that should not be played by wizard's apprentices. There is hardly any scope for regulation of the system for excellence and social commitment. But there is a regulatory role of the State and the university in curbing naked commercialization. Unless the condition of the requisite infrastructure and inputs, necessary for teaching and learning are met by the private institutions, they should not be recognized by and affiliated to the university. Before giving permission for starting a college, an institute or a private university, to an agency or an organization, the government should ascertain the socio-economic background, moral status and educational fidelity of the applicant. Permission granted conditionally should have a clause of strict scrutiny and verification by academicians of repute and firm moral and educational commitment. "Only an active regulation of the State clarifying and endorsing the rules of the system can make it possible to take complete advantage of the introduction of the market like mechanism. Any other position of the State will drive the higher education to a complicated course. (Amaral and Teixeira, 2000)". In fact, at the moment, what is urgently needed is blending of the best features of outstanding private institutions into the public institutions of higher education. Besides, the public must respect the underlying values of higher education. The governments and public authorities should come forward to give universities the protective support they need to fulfill their mission.

## References

Altbach, Philip G. Higher Education and the WTO : Globalization Run Amok. *University News*, 39 (37), 1-4, 2001.

Amaral, Alberto and Teixeira, Pedro. The Rise and fall of the Private sector in Portuguese Higher Education. *Higher Education Policy*, 13, 2000.

Bakshi, Rajni. Beyond Market Fundamentalism. *The Hindu : Sunday Magazine*. September 24, 2000.

Baldwin, G. The Student as Customer: The Discourse of Quality in Higher Education. *Journal of Tertiary Education Administration*, 16(1), 125-133, 1994.

Blair, Tony. *Romanes Lecture*. University of Oxford, December 2, 1999.

Delors, Jacques (Chair). *Learning: The Treasure Within (Report* to UNESCO of International Commission of Education for 21st Century), 1996.

Durant, Will. *The Pleasures of Philosophy*. New York: Simon and Schuster, 1981.

Sethi, J.D., *The Crisis and Collapse of Higher Education in India*. New Delhi: Vikas Publishing House, 1987.

Shotten, John Robert, *Learning and Freedom*. New Delhi: Sage Publication, 1998.

Singh, Nirmal. *Education under seize*. New Delhi: Concept Publication, 1983.

Tilak, J.B.G. Myths and Facts about Privatization of Higher Education. *Journal of Higher Education*, 6 (2), Spring, 1993.

# 20

# Modern Education System: An Overhaul Needed

Education is preeminently a social thing in its origin and function. "What nutrition and reproduction are to physiological life," says John Dewey, "education is to social life." The process of education is organized and executed to draw out the best in child and man on the one hand and to regulate order and change in the society on the other. Education has the power to promote mobility and mutation in the society. The soundness of any system of education is determined by the quality and creativity of its product. Reports of various organizations, boards and commissions and finding of occasional surveys reveal that, in general, standards of education are deteriorating. A majority of youngsters who have earned university degrees are not found fit even for clerical jobs. Some of them are found unemployable due to their deficiency and weakness in the basics of education. A concerted concern for identification and development of talent and creativity in youth is also missing in educational institutions of the country. The system of education is not only iniquitous and dualistic but openly pitted against the poor. We have excellence at the top and mediocrity really worthwhile at the bottom. We have a fair number of quality schools in the country, but unlike the US, no world-class universities other than the IITs. In a study conducted by the World economic Forum, in the past on the global competitiveness of nations, it was revealed that of 53 countries surveyed India ranked 53rd on linkages between academia and Industry.

As an exception, two scenarios stand out to demonstrate the strength of the present education system that was instituted by the British. Firstly, it is very often said that the Indians who participated in the struggle for independence of the country and won freedom were the product of this non-indigenous system of education. The same system had produced two 'Noble Laureates' before independence. Secondly, the Silicon Valley Indian start-up gurus and stars, in their interviews with Gurmeet Naroola (2001)* have acknowledged that the education, habit of hard work and family system of the country have made a significant contribution in enabling them to excel and to build their company empires in the USA in spite of all obstacles and competitiveness. Here, it must be stated that almost all of these 25 entrepreneurs were the pass outs of the IITs and IIMs which are counted as world class institutions and they are not a part of the British educational legacy.

One thing is very clear about both the events that the individuals concerned were placed in 'do or die' type of situation which created an extraordinary drive in them to employ their entire repertoire of talent and creativity in accomplishing their cherished goals. If we like, may treat the above stated events as 'exceptional cases'. But, in general, the students of our educational institutions are found lacking in their performance in various examinations and selection tests. Like the proverbial 'tail' wagging the 'dog', the ritual of examinations has been

---

* Naroola, Gurmeet : *The Entrepreneurial Connection*. New Delhi : Tata McGraw-Hill Publishing Co. Ltd., 2001.

successful in subordinating the entire system of education of the country. Excepting some world-class institutions, most of the educational institutions are degenerating rapidly for want of funds and recruitment of competent and dedicated teachers. To overcome the handicap of 'resource crunch', self-financed courses and privatization of education were encouraged. Lack of financial and academic discipline has brought a bad name to these courses. Eight myths about privatization of higher education have been exploded by research studies. These myths mostly relate to the claim of superiority of private higher education in terms of input, output, quality, internal efficiency and employment, rate of social return, research, profit-motive equality and politicization.

We live in the times of change and obsolescence. Rapidity of change puts strain and stress not only on individuals' physical capacity and decision-making ability but also on various subsystems of the society. Political, economic and educational subsystems are also affected by the pace of social change to the extent that, in some cases, they get disoriented. During times of change and transience a wide spread discontent with existing social system and social institutions is witnessed in almost all modern societies. To cope with the new situations, created by change, people expect educational institutions to impart newer knowledge, skills and attitudes to the new generation. It is in the nature of change to 'create complexity, uncertainty and emergency in the existing social and institutional setup. These unsettling tendencies can be confronted successfully, if through the educational system, the mind set of the youth is made creative, flexible and receptive. The present day education system and institutions, therefore, need to be reorganized and reequipped to offset the crash landing of the youth in future. In a nutshell, education must shift into future tense.

The Indian education system has been diagnosed and remedies for reform have been suggested by different commissions, committees and conferences, from time to time, since the day India was liberated from British domination. Latest in the series of such important documents is the national policy on education (1986), which was later on reviewed by a committee in 1992 and an Action Plan was drawn for implementation. The essence or consensus of almost all of such recommendations made so far, for reforming or overhauling the education system, can be summed up into the following themes.

1. Democratization and decentralization of educational administration at all levels.
2. Periodic reconstruction of curriculum to update the contents.
3. Induction of an open, participative and creative climate of teaching and learning in the educational institutions.
4. Inculcation of values indispensable for creation of an enlightened and humane society.
5. Sciene research and productive work as basic components of education.
6. Acceptance of equality, access, quality, innovativeness and futuristic orientation as guiding principles in overall organization and administration of education.
7. Continuous evaluation through semester and grading system.
8. Identification and development of talent and creativity.
9. Recruitment of 'edupreneurs' as teachers who can visualize ideas and strategies that impact industry and education.
10. Ensuring availability of better teachers and facilities in the rural, tribal and slum areas to bridge the gap between urban and rural higher education.
11. An efficient mechanism should be evolved to regulate and control privatization of higher education to ensure standard and quality.
12. Quality in higher education can not be ensured until and unless quality of primary and secondary stages of education are adequately improved.

# 21

# Raising Quality of Higher Education

Excepting a very few world-class institutes like IITs, IIMs and IISc, standard or quality of higher education in our country has deteriorated abysmally in the past few decades. This has been repeatedly pointed out by the public service commissions, companies and many other testing and recruiting agencies. These organizations have gone to the extent of saying that hardly 10 to 15% pass-outs of the universities and colleges are found suitable for employment. I think, at least six major causes are visible and responsible for the decline of higher education:

1. An unprecedented lack of resources,
2. Under-performance and indifference of teachers and researchers to quality,
3. Paucity of thoughtfulness and initiative on the part of educational administrators to find out alternative ways cooperatively to tackle the crisis of quality in higher education,
4. A dearth of love for higher learning and lust for knowledge in majority of the students,

5. A myth propagated by petty politicians that ends can be achieved by employing foul means, and
6. Political patronage to non-performers.

Higher education, no doubt is in a shambles and its collapse is almost complete. In the year 1983, in the book: *The Crisis and Collapse of Higher Education in India*, Late J.D. Sethi, has made a drastic observation that "unless the whole structure of higher education is changed, nothing really worthwhile could be achieved. We have excellence at the top and nothing really worthwhile at the bottom. This situation will continue as long as fundamental changes are not made in higher education first. The situation has long passed the stage of reforms." Therefore, the task of restoring quality to higher education is stupendous, but it is not impossible.

Scientists have been able to awaken life in the fossils. It requires an unflinching resolve on the part of the teachers and educational leaders to stem the rot, and to put higher education on the pedestal. This can be done because a teacher plays a paramount role as a transactor of curricula and interventor of the whole process of higher learning and teaching. Teacher is a builder of the stellar of quality. The deficit of resources can also be compensated or overcome to a great extent by his innovative ideas and resourcefulness. It is said that during the time of economic depression the great physicist Prof. Lord Rutherford, on finding his fellow-scientists and researchers in panic, asked them to spend thoughts when they don't have money to invest.

Quality is neither a substance, nor a method. It is a goal towards which method is aimed. Quality is the continuing stimulus which causes us to diagnose and redirect our performance to identify and eliminate deficiencies and deformations. Quality consciousness is related to the total work environment. Precisely, it is aimed at improving the standard of the inputs and the process of teaching; learning and evaluation, to finally make the achievement of the students nationally and internationally comparable.

There are some people who feel that quality is a characteristic of thought and statement that is recognized by a non-thinking process, because definitions are a product of rigid, formal thinking. The world can function without quality, but life would be so dull as to be hardly worth living. The term 'worth' is a quality term. Since the world obviously does not function normally when quality is subtracted. Quality exists, whether it is defined or not. When you subtract quality you get squareness. Absence of quality is the essence of squareness. Existence of quality can be seen empirically in the classroom, and can be demonstrated logically by showing that a world, without it can not exist as we know it. Quality is just the focal point around which a lot of intellectual furniture is getting rearranged.

Quality could not be independently related with either the subject or the object, but could be found only in the interrelationship of the two with each other. Quality is not a thing. It is an event. It is the event at which the subject becomes aware of the object. Quality is the parent, the source of all subjects and objects. Quality is the response of an organism to its environment. We, having a developed nervous system, would act in a much more complex way than an amoeba, to overcome the poor quality of the environment. Quality is the continuing stimulus which our environment puts upon us to create the world in which we live. Quality is not something you lay on top of subjects and objects like 'tinsel' on a Christmas tree. Real quality must be the source of the subjects and objects, the cone from which the tree must start.

In any task as simple as sharpening a pencil or as complex as producing a novel painting, the underlying problems are the same. In each case there is a beautiful way of doing it and an ugly way of doing it. In arriving at the high-quality, beautiful way of doing it, both an ability to see what "looks good" and an ability to understand the underlying methods to arrive at that "good" are needed. Both classic and romantic understanding of quality must be combined. 'Peace of mind' is a prerequisite for a perception of the quality. The way to see what looks good and understand the reason it looks good, and to be at one with this goodness as the work proceeds, is to cultivate an inner quietness, a peace of mind so that goodness can shine through. This inner peace of mind occurs on three levels of understanding. 'Physical quietness', seems the easiest to achieve, although there are levels and levels of this too, as attested by the ability of Hindu mystics to live buried alive for many days. 'Mental quietness', in which one has no wandering thoughts at all, seems more difficult, but can be achieved. But 'value quietness', in which one has no wandering desires at all but simply performing the acts of his life without desire, that seems the hardest.

A quality conscious worker or a professional has an intense feeling for the work. There is no sense of separateness from what he or she is working on. In this state of mind one can be said to "care" about what is he or she is doing. This type of caring and intimate involvement, finally develops in the worker an identification with the work. Thus, the key to quality performance or excellent work, is the feeling of oneness with the work.

## Quality of Higher Education

Quality in the context of management has been defined by Philip Crosby as "Conformance to requirements", and in the context of education by D. Green as : "fitness for purpose". The 'requirements' or 'purposes' are usually included in the, mission statements' and 'objectives' of the institutions. In my opinion quality is continuous and consistence high performance. In other words, we can say that quality is almost synonymous with excellence.

In is rightly said that quality has much in common with beauty. Everyone is for it, but unfortunately everyone does not work for it. Infact, quality problems are non-conformance problems. Quality is measured, according to Crosby, by "cold hard cash". This is infact an expense of non-conformance. Said differently, the cost of doing things wrong or 'not -doing things right the first time" is the cost of quality. In Crosby's words the costs are divided into prevention, appraisal and failure categories. Therefore, the organizations or the institutions have to be vaccinated against non-conformance to the standards or specified requirements stated as objectives. Crosby thinks that the institutions can be provided with antibodies, in the form of managerial actions some of which are procedural common sense. Three distinct managerial actions, namely, determination, education and implementation are needed to be combined to prepare the vaccine to prevent non-conformance and non-performance.

Since all the stages of education: primary, secondary and tertiary are interdependent, quality of one stage of education can not be conceived and considered in isolation of the other. Efforts for qualitative improvement must be started from the primary stage of education. Any deficiency incurred or tolerated at the initial stage will get reflected in the later stages, and then it will be more difficult and time consuming to eliminate it. Quality is the cumulative effect of the activities of all the participant components of the process. In higher education it is the result of the combined efforts of the administration, the teacher, the students and the parents. Here the teacher has a bigger role to play as he is required to make interventions while transacting curriculum by employing variety of aids and resources. Diagnostic and remedial teaching has been found very much useful in strengthening the strength and weakening the weakness of the learner.

The responsibility of quality enhancement and sustenance, in the area of higher education, can not be solely left to the National Assessment and Accreditation Council (NAAC). Its past record is not commendable. It has, knowingly or unknowingly, reduced the whole exercise of assessment and accreditation to a mechanical ritual. Visits of its peer teams, constituted for assessment of colleges and universities, have taken the form of a ceremonial activity. It has failed to inspire and motivate the teachers and administrators of the institutions to innovate teaching practices and to give new directions to research and extension services. Infact, quality improvement programme has to be promoted as a crusade or a movement against the deteriorating standards of higher education. Rising tide of mediocrity is a big threat to the future of resurgent India. The eleventh five year plan has rightly envisaged employment of a private agency for the purpose of assessment and accreditation.

Teaching and research, known as the two basic components of higher education have been degenerated in to a dull and mechanical ritual. The class room has become a 'lesson hearing room' in which the games of 'stamp collection of facts' and of getting an exact answer are played. The students have become passive consumers of facts, and they have ceased to be active investigator of ideas. To induct quality in the teaching and learning process, teachers' initiative, innovativeness and enterprising attitude must be revived and reinforced. Only then, the classroom would become a fertile ground for employing inquiry and discovery methods of teaching and learning to enable learners to reconstruct their experience and construct knowledge by themselves.

It is said that if you want your teachers to be imaginative, ask them to do research. No doubt, research keeps a teacher intellectually trim, and it acts as an antidote to intellectual death. It refreshes both the 'research-teacher' and the 'teacher-researcher'. But, again, emphasis could be misplaced if teachers run after the latest fashion and frills, for doing research, instead of concentrating on what is genuinely required to be researched, to tackle the day-to-day problems and to examine the fundamentals of teaching and learning in view of the changing national and international scenario. Unfortunately, a chasm between teaching and research has been created since the day the research activity had acquired glamour and snob-value. Hence, a balance has to be striked between the acts of teaching and research.

For sustaining and enhancing quality the two innovations, namely, 'Institutional Planning' and 'College Complex or cluster' recommended by the Kothari Education Commission (1964-66) are still relevant to be practiced. They have not been given sufficient and sincere trial so far. The idea of institutional planning is very simple and convincing. An outline of yearly plan and programme of the institution need to be prepared and all activities of college or a university teaching department have to be conducted according to this road map. Since the plan is prepared cooperatively and on the basis of consensus of the teachers, it will act as an instrument of evolving 'team spirit' and a mutually supportive ethos for its implementation. Similarly, the problem of scarcity of aids, equipment, and technical know-how can be easily overcome by forming a clusters or fraternity of a few colleges, making them the forums for periodic sharing of ideas, practices and equipments. Such an initiative has been taken by the progressive private and central schools under the banner of 'sahodaya', and it is engaging the attention of the educators. I am sure, these inexpensive and easy to implement innovations, would go a long way in ameliorating the poor condition of teaching, learning and research in the colleges and universities.

For raising the quality of higher education, I would also like to place before you the idea of 'style of life' advanced by A.N. Whitehead. In this approach to life and work, the worker or the practitioner is expected to avoid wastefulness, to economize material, and to prefer good work. Here, an emphasis has been laid on parsimonious use of materials and perhaps that is why, this attitude to work, is addressed as an 'ultimate morality of mind' and the 'last acquirement of an educated person', by the late philosopher, mathematician and educationist A.N.Whitehead.

Friends, I know we are all highly educated people and we perhaps don't welcome sermons. But still, I would like to emphasize that in these days when the society is being driven by knowledge, competition and market, quality higher education has become a condition of survival for all of us. What is lacking in our institutional ethos is the 'team spirit' and 'determination' to execute the ideas we value. Preservation and enhancement of quality, undoubtedly is one of those noble and valuable ideas. Let us come together, keep together and work together to make this idea a reality. Higher education is so important in the 21st century that it can not be left to chance. It is the only process through which we can prepare such a lot of young people "who are easy to lead but difficult to drive, easy to govern but impossible to enslave". To attain this goal, I would like to share with you, in the end, our prime minister Dr. Manmohan Singh's following valuable words: "We can not make higher education a prisoner of either bureaucracy or ideology. It must develop on the foundation of professional excellence and intellectual integrity". No doubt, the ultimate determinant of quality is the sense of deep and active involvement with the work, and a drive to demonstrate an excellent performance inside and outside the classroom to enable the students to actualize their potential.

# 22

# Value Orientation in Higher Education

We live in a turbulent time and an unstable present. The past is fast receding. The future is arriving prematurely creating cataclysmic changes and disorientation in the society. This situation of rapidity of change expects of those who work in the institutions of higher education to guide change, and to reshape the attitudes and beliefs of the youth to facilitate emergence of new norms and values to substitute the replacable old ones. Even in such a time of upheaval, the privileged class of the society is seen complacent and indifferent towards its responsibility of filling in the void created by premature arrival of the future. At times, this part of the population is found lost in the pleasures of self-love and affluence. They rarely give thought to the problems of nearly 70% of Indians who are disprivileged, and of 30% for whom even filling of their bellies is getting increasingly harder day-by-day.

The soul of the nation long suppressed has not yet been able to find opportunity for utterance. No doubt, science and technology have multiplied material facilities and transformed the world into a 'global village' through speedy means of transport and telecommunication. However, a need is felt, to humanize science and technology so that they are not employed "to kill in wholesale and heal in retail". Unfortunately, the fruits of science and technology have not reached to the poor people living in the remote rural and tribal areas. Earlier, Swami Vivekanand had rightly warned the intelligentsia in his speeches that "the talk of economic growth and social reform had little meaning if it was confined to a small society of urban middle class. So long as millions live in hunger and ignorance, I hold every man a traitor who having been educated at their expense pays not the least heed to them".

Keeping in mind Swamiji's remark, let us hurry-up to re-examine and to redefine our developmental policies, priorities and value judgements to make available the benefits of science, technology, research and education to the poorest of the poor in the country. Let us be very clear about our idea of progress and development. 'Techno-economic-growth' oriented approach to progress and modernity has grown into the 'measles of mankind'. Economic policy and reform, therefore, should not be allowed to deform and divide society to ultimately turn it into an unsustainable society. A holistic and symbiotic approach to reform is the need of the hour. Long before, the 'Club of Rome' raised its voice in favour of the 'limits of growth', Gandhiji in the year 1916, in his lecture to the students of Allahabad University posed the question 'Is economic progress a real progress ?' He himself answered the question: "by economic progress we mean material advancement without limit, and by real progress we mean moral progress" (Chaudhari, 2001). In the present world, spoiled by market fundamentalism and consumerism, we urgently need to have a paradigm shift towards the Gandhian approach to progress, development and modernity. "Indifference", says Dr. Dayakrishna (1998), "is the sign of immorality. One ought to be disturbed, and if one is not so disturbed at the suffering of others, then, one is not a human being. The development of thick skinned consciousness which is not disturbed by what it ought to be disturbed is, in the moral perspective, not a sign of development but of dehumanization".

Socrates believed that the "fundamental structure of human nature is constant, therefore, certain moral values are constant". But, in the third decade of twentieth century, Will Durant (1980) analyzed the social situation and said: "Morals which change so slowly, are changing today like clouds before the wind". Elaborating his analysis further he observed: "It is the age of Socrates again: our moral life is threatened and our intellectual life is quickened and enlarged by the disintegration of ancient customs and beliefs. Everything is new and experimental in our ideas and our actions; nothing is established or certain any more.. .All things flow and we are at a loss to find some moorings and stability in the flux... Our culture is superficial today, and our knowledge is dangerous, because we are rich in mechanisms today and poor in purposes. The balance of mind, which once came of a warm religious faith, is gone; science has taken from us the supernatural basis of morality, and all the world seems consumed in a disorderly individualism that reflects the chaotic fragmentation of our character... Without philosophy, without the total vision which unifies purposes and establishes the hierarchy of desires, we fritter away our social heritage in cynical corruption on the one hand, and in revolutionary madness on the other; we abandon in a moment our pacific idealism and plunge into cooperative suicide of war; we have a hundred thousand politicians, and not a single statesman. We move about the earth with unprecedented speed, but we do not know, and have not thought, where we are going, or whether we shall find any happiness there for our harassed souls. We are being destroyed by our knowledge, which has made us drunk with our power. And we shall not be saved without wisdoms."

Can we pin our hopes on higher education to remedy the malady of lack of holistic view and moral inertia? Perhaps yes.

A large number of thinkers and philosophers, including Aurobindo and Vivekanand pronounced their verdict in favour of the process of education since human beings have tremendous potential for good and immense inclination for morality. Infact this dimension of human beings has not been sincerely harnessed and nurtured to evolve them as 'homo-morals' through socialization and education. While defining education as the process by which man becomes man, Kant put forth his opinion that: "the peculiarity of truly human life is that man has to make himself truly moral, rational and free being. This creative effort is carried on by the educational activities of slow generations. Its acceleration depends on men consciously striving to educate their successors not for existing state of affairs but so as to make possible a future better humanity". John Dewey also supports this thesis by saying that man should discover and choose his morals like facts.

The rational man has to grow into the spiritual man. This is the task set before each individual if he is to fulfill his destiny as a human being. This is the essence of philosophy and science. The deepest indictment of the university is that it erodes religious and spiritual belief. Modernity is also blamed for triggering loss of faith in transcendence. K. Satchidananda Murty (1991) has rightly remarked: "Let not our universities lead our youth into such 'nihilistic Sahara'. The alternative to nihilism is religion". What is expected of institutions of higher education in the modern times is to create a climate and a setting for the emergence of the moral and spiritual urge in the youth through informal and co-curricular programmes involving free interaction and inquiry. In this regard, philosopher and management guru Charles Handy's words could be of great value. He says: "soul is one of those concepts that like beauty is instantly recognizable when you meet it. Organizations have a feel about them, a feel which the visitor picks up as soon as he or she enters the building or, often, merely encounters one of the people who work there" (Kamat, 2002). This statement implies that an institution of higher learning can best serve the society by giving a feel of 'model society' within itself, and one whose primary concern is : 'good of the students is good for man' (Sanford, 1969). So, in universities the communication of trust, love, truth and freedom need the going concern of scholarship, in which these values function in university life. An active orientation towards participatory concern is needed for affectivity and a relationship of trust.

It is said and rightly said that values are caught and not taught. In his scheme of moral education, Shri Aurobindo also showed preference for indirect methods. According to him the first rule of moral training was to suggest and invite, not command or impose. "The best methods of suggestions are by personal example, daily converse and the books read from day to day. These books should contain for the younger students, the lofty examples of the past given not as moral lessons, but as things of supreme human interest, and for the elder student, the great thoughts of great souls, the passages of literature which set fire to the highest ideals and aspirations, the records of history and biography which exemplify the living of those great thoughts, noble emotions and aspiring ideals. This is a kind of good company, 'Satsang', which can seldom fail to have effect so long as sententious sermonizing is avoided, and becomes of the highest effect if the personal life of the teachers is itself moulded by the great things he places before his pupils. It can not however, have full force unless the young life is given an opportunity within its limited sphere of embodying in action the moral impulses which rise within it". Thus the students must have plenty of opportunity to habituate themselves to moral ideals and value judgements. Put differently, the only way to learn 'fair play' is to play fair. Moral learning in the universities and colleges must be continuous with moral learning outside, through field trips, community activities, social services and the like. Then, anything learned in an undertaking having an aim in cooperation with others, will be inevitably moral.

"Teaching for character formation (or moral development) in higher education", say Mckeon (1969), does not depend on the addition of new arts and disciplines to those proper to higher education. It does depend, however, on fuller use of the arts of interpretation, discovery, presentation and systemization, and an understanding of their bearing on the person who acquires them, as well as, their bearing on the subject matters on which they are practiced."

Pt. Nehru is his convocation address to the University of Allahabad in 1947, elucidating the role of a university, has said: "a university stands for humanism, for tolerance, for reason, for the adventure of ideas and for the search of truth. It stands for the onward march of the human race towards even higher objectives". These human and academic values named here can be realized by making university an open and dialogical forum for debate and discussion. Infact, a university is only the place where accepted practices, dogmas and doctrines can be questioned with impunity. It is in such an open and free atmosphere, which allows 'clash of doctrines' to occur, novel ideas are originated, and "through 'human-smithy' character is forged in the furnace of experience and beaten on the anvil of truth" (Curzon, 1903). A social context of this quality will go a long way in making universities work like communities within which commonalities are respected and differences are appreciated with brimming affectivity and trust.

Education is a moral enterprise, and hence no educational knowledge can be autonomous and value-free. We are living in a knowledge-driven society where power is shifting towards knowledge. In this situation, if knowledge is left unguided, there is every possibility of its being abused for manipulating and domesticating people. It is a truism to say that ignorance with goodness is futile, and knowledge devoid of values is dangerous. This has been amply demonstrated by the phenomenon of environmental degradation, violence, crime, AIDS and widespread corruption in the society. Since democracy is based on the intelligence, creativity and dignity of the individuals, efforts must be·made in the universities and colleges to depreciate the tendency of 'by-standers' antipathy' and 'passive goodness' by infusing in the youth the spirit of 'moral rage' and of offering resistance to attempts on the part of the people in authority to use citizens as tools. Higher education in a democracy must aim at preparing young people who are "Easy to lead but difficult to drive, easy to govern but impossible to enslave".

One of the most significant aspects of our current situation is "the crisis of meaning. Perspectives in life and the world, often of a scientific temper, have so proliferated that we face an increasing fragmentation of knowledge. This makes the search for meaning difficult and often fruitless. A philosophy that no longer asks the question of the meaning of life would be in grave danger of reducing reason to merely accessory functions, with no real passion for the search for truth (Jhon Paul II, quoted by Bricall, 2000)." This is a challenge for the universities, which are responsible for researching and disseminating truth and also for assessing the consequences of new knowledge. A university is known as the 'conscience' of the society. Therefore, its duty is not primarily to give society what it wants, but what it needs. Unless universities have an ambition to make an impact on the quality of social thinking, they will not be able to help in the renewal of the society to cherish flexible and creative habits, attitudes and values so that the individuals are enabled to cope with uncertainties and emergencies arising out of complex and changing times. The universities can play their role efficiently and effectively in the times of change if they decide to promote constructive and creative disagreement in political and academic matters, and encourage men and women to question dispassionately the outworn practices and vested interests. Undoubtedly such a pursuit needs, above all, in the words of the Kothari Commission (1964-66) "courage and fearlessness. Great universities and timid people go ill together".

As we move into the third millennium, there is reason to believe that in this era of post-modernity we will see a major breakthrough toward dialogue between faith and world. Among the tendencies to lead us closer in the philosophical inquiry into our relational nature with the other, and a new religious model in which the idea of filiation as a fundamental paradigm is renewed. "Many modern and contemporary authors look for the dignity of human person in the person's capacity to establish inter-subjective relationships of knowledge and love with other human beings, and in forming a community with humanity. A new humanism must recognize an "Infinite Being' with whom each human person is called to enter in communion and through whom the human person realizes an analogous relationship with infinite dignity (Melady, 2000)".

In the end, I invite your attention to the concept of the 'perennial tension' highlighted by the report to UNESCO of International Commission on Education for the 21st century (1996) titled as *Learning : The Treasure within* under the chair of Jacques Delors. The perennial tension is seen as a disharmony between the spiritual and the material aspects of life. Exampling this concept, the report says: "Often without realizing it, the world has a longing, often expressed, for an ideal and for values that we shall term moral. It is thus education's noble task to encourage each and every one, acting in accordance with their traditions and convictions, and paying full respect to pluralism, to lift their minds and spirits to the plane of the universal, and in some measure, to transcend themselves. It is no exaggeration on the commission's part to say that the survival of the humanity depends thereon". To me it appears that this concern for the 'perennial tension' can be settled if the age old Indian ideal of accepting the whole earth as our family is revived, respected and promoted: अयं निजः परोवेति गणना लघुचेतसां उदार चरितानाम् तु वसुधैव कुटुंबकं" This means: "small minded people talk in terms of this is mine and that is their but for the generous and large hearted people, the whole earth is a family".

## References

Bricall, Joseph. 'Some Recent Trends in the Universities'. University of Barcelona, Catalonia, Spain, 2000.

Chaudhari, Kamala, 'Progress Redifined'. *Madhya Pradesh Journal of Social Sciences,* 6 (1), January-June 2001.

Curzon, Lord. *Convocation Address* to Calcutta University, 1903.

Dayakrishna. *Social Philosophy: Past and Future*, 1998.

Delors, J. *Learning: The Treasure Within*, Report to UNESCO of the International Commission on Education, for the Twenty-first Century, 1996.

Durant, Will. *The Pleasure of Philosophy*. New York: Simon and Schuster, 1981.

Kamat, Vinay. 'The Ethical Corporation'. *Times of India,* February 7, 2002.

Mckeon, Richard. 'Character and the Arts and Disciplines'. In Faust C. H . and Feingold J. (ed), *Approaches to Education for Character*. N.Y. : Columbia University Press. 1969.

Melady, Margaret. Presentation in the Conference on the Human Person: Genealogy, Biology and Biography. American University of Rome, Italy, 2000.

Murty, Satchidanand. *Ethics, Education, Indian Unity and Culture*, Delhi: Ajanta Publications, 1991.

*Report of the Education Commission (1964-66).* Delhi: Ministry of Education, Govt. of India, 1966.

Sanford, Nevitt. 'The Contribution of Higher Education to the life of Society.' In Niblett W.R. (cd), *Higher Education - Demand and Response.* London: Travistock Publications, 1969.

# 23

# Education and Social Change

Amongst various other things, a teacher is expected to be an agent of social change. In the past, education has had primarily a conservative function, that of transmitting a relatively unchanging culture and traditional skills to the new generation. Only in a changing society, or one seeking to change, can education play a role in the introduction of change.

## Concept of Social Change

In the popular mind everything that changes within the society constitutes 'social change', from variation in the patterns of fashion to movements in population and general scientific advance. But, social change does not merely imply a structural and functional change in the organizations, norms and roles of society, it also implies a change in its cultural system, beliefs, ideals, traditions and practices.

Social change is a transforming process. The word 'process' implies the idea of continuity, and social change is certainly something that is perpetually happening, and in a variety of ways. However, nothing is said here about the quality, good or bad, of the process, it is simply a way of describing how things happen in a society, and also the way in which people adapt to certain elements in their society, or they assimilate certain forms of activity, or adjust themselves to specific modes of behaviour. At the same time, the educated and enlightened section of the society has an obligation to regulate the change according to the readiness of the people to cope with it.

**Factors of Social Change:**

Change is inevitable in life and society. In the simpler societies change has been rare and usually slow, caused by culture contact or by such disasters as wars, epidemics and famines. In a more complex society, it may be caused by internal revolution and civil strife as in Russia, by emancipatory efforts to attain self-governance as it happened in some of the new African states, by increased inventiveness such as the discovery of something like 'atomic energy' and 'Internet', or by the impact of a great leader like 'Mahatma Gandhi' or 'Marx'.

Social change can be caused by three main types of factors, namely, physical and biological, technological; and cultural (MacIver and Page, 1950). In any attempt to explain the causation of social change, it is possible to select one particular factor and overemphasize it. Thus, Huttington (1919, 1924) held that the determining environment of geography and climate was responsible for social change; for Karl Marx (1930), the determining factors which were of paramount importance were economic, whilst, several others have argued that technological advances also push forward the social changes. But, the more one considers the causation of social change, the more one gets involved with the complex nature of society. As Morrish (1972) has so aptly stated "the web of social relationships which we call society is reticulated and intersected by almost every technical invention, every vagary of fashion or art form, every new technique of birth control and every increase of efficiency in the means of production or social control. Life is one, and the change experienced in social relationship is both the cause and effect".

Education is a conscious process of attaining self-awareness and social awareness. It tends to transform both the individual and the society through progressive manifestation of knowledge. Education and social change are interrelated concepts. Social change is the end product of education but at the same time social change presses upon the value trends in education to generate new concepts and innovative ideas, which are again passed on to the society to stimulate change.

**Role of Education**

In the past, education has had primarily a conservative function, of transmitting the cultural heritage, as it is to the young generation, in the form of traditional knowledge, skill and attitudes. In the modern society, education is expected to perform the change function by updating and renewing the knowledge, skills and disposition suitable to the changing society:

(i) *Preservation of the cultural heritage by transmitting it to the next generation:* Consequently, schools are expected to inculcate the dominant value system of the society. Education also helps the individuals to examine and edit the heritage and to eliminate that part which is not found serviceable in the modern times.

(ii) *Agencies of social reform or social improvement:* In post-independence period, the schools were asked to prepare the students to play their role in the emerging Indian society by shedding the colonial past. Thus, in our country, after 1947 an emphasis was laid on initiating the children and youth in national consciousness, democratic attitude and scientific spirit.

(iv) *Encouraging innovation in the socio-economic and scientific technological sphere:* This may involve the process of thinking differently and discovering new ways of creating and adding value to products and services.

Imaginative consideration of knowledge has been accepted as the objective of higher education. Emphasis is being placed on informed acceptance of ideas, flexible attitude and creative approach to change for humanizing technology of tomorrow.

**Cultural Lag**

Education, while seeking to preserve and transmit the cultural heritage of the society, must also try and ensure that as little 'cultural lag' as possible occurs within the society. This means that there must be some attempt to reform the old beliefs and mind-set to be receptive to new conditions and ways of life so that individuals may keep up with scientific and technological changes occurring in the society. Ogburn and Nimkoff (1960) have summed up the situation in the following words: "When culture begins to change, the modifications do not occur evenly in all parts of the social heritage. Some parts change faster than others. When the different parts are interrelated, the varying rates of change produce a strain between the unequally moving parts. That part which is moving at the 'slowest rate' of speed constitutes the 'cultural lag'. Since the other parts of the culture have already changed, as a rule, the most practicable method of effecting a better integration between the two parts is to make some adjustment in the part that is lagging". Modern technology is changing at a rapid rate and creating important changes, with which our social institutions have not yet kept pace. Analysis of important modern social problems, such as unemployment, poverty, family disorganization and generation gap shows that much of our contemporary social disorganization issues from the irregular change of our culture.

**Social Change in Relation to Education**

The 'cultural lag' is apparent in the curricula being taught in the schools and colleges. To remedy this, the way in which teachers are prepared for their profession must also change.

Emphasis must be placed on comprehensive education which demands the development of an 'all round approach to the pupil'. Efforts should also be made to develop 'social insight' and 'sociological imagination' in the prospective teachers. In the 'all round approach; the intellectual progress of the pupils is regarded as of less importance, than the broadening of their horizons and interests generally, and the development of their awareness and understanding of other human beings. The present emphasis according to Mannheim (1940), should no longer be upon 'instruction and learning' but rather on development of 'living'. He suggested that we must seek in education to provide a curriculum which is firmly based on the social situation of the learners, in which is involved the pattern of inherited culture, the unique content of contemporary culture and the culture of the foreseen future. Mannheim (1940) has also stressed the importance of developing a sense of common purpose between the home, the school, and the society. Considering further the problem of social change in relation to education, Mannheim is of the opinion that the teachers should be educated in a way which would enable them to understand the meaning and implications of change for education and social development.

Current social change indicates an increasing demand for innovation and adaptability, and therefore all forms of education must clearly have these aspects in view. Ronald Gould (1967), has warned that mechanical and industrial changes make greater and greater demands on individuals, and education needs to pull itself together and make quite sure that it meets the needs of modern society. In a rapidly changing society, educators have to be keenly aware of change, but education must not just go along with it. Change must be evaluated and directed, and education must encourage the right kind of innovation that match the preparedness and capability of people.

However, Durkheim (1952, 1956) holds a deterministic view of society. He argues that it is not the aim of education to present some picture of an 'ideal society' to the child. Nor is it the object of the educationist to consider some ideal form of education for such a society. He further goes on to state that "to the extent that real life increasingly takes possession of him (the child), it will come to destroy the work of the teacher. Education, therefore, can be reformed only if society itself is reformed". Again, he insists that education is only 'the image and reflection of society', it imitates and reproduces the latter in an abbreviated form, but it does not create it. Thus, it would seem, according to Durkheim, that the educational system alone can change neither society nor itself.

But, how can society reform itself, except through some means, agent or institution such as education? It would seem a reasonable assumption that, any nation, which has a vision of some more desirable society, will seek to realize that vision, atleast, through its educational system. Therefore, there is, and must be, an interaction between education and society. It is not just a one way process, as Durkheim appears to imply, but the institution and process of education can in turn, change and modify the social structure. Though, developments within education are influenced considerably by economic and technological factors, education may also influence, social and economic factors directly as a consequence of its role in the discovery and dissemination of new knowledge through research. The spread of education and the organization of educational institutions may have important social consequences for attitudes, values and belief system of a society.

**Education and Economic Development**

There was a widespread belief in education being the main determinant of economic growth. If education is a root, economic growth is the fruit, and vice-versa. However, it has been found that in its relationship to the occupational structure, education is likely to be a dependent rather than an independent variable. The connection between education and economic growth is a complex one. Thus, Bowman and Anderson (1963), found little economic development in countries with less than 30 per cent literacy rate, and a literacy rate of over 90 per cent in countries with the highest per capita income, but there was no clear correlation to be found, for countries falling between the above two extremes. Hoselitz (1968), confirms that the productive aspect of education is applicable only to advanced countries, like U.S.A. and Western Europe. These conditions apply only to a limited extent, if at all, to developing countries.

This, however, does not mean that education has no impact whatsoever on economic development. Indeed, there is some evidence to suggest that an educated population is an asset of considerable importance to a country anxious to catch up with a more advanced economy. Musgrave (1967) is, of the opinion, that the efficiency of her educational system enabled Germany to catch up with Britain after initially late take-off into industrialization. Dore (1965) too claims that a high literacy rate in the 1870's was an important factor in the swift development of Japan as a highly industrialized nation.

On the other hand, educational expansion that outstrips occupational needs, results in educational devaluation, as has happened in some developing countries. But, education performs another important role by introducing the developing society to new needs, new expectations and even to the idea of change itself. Education helps to wean the developing society away from the old, and towards the new. It inspires a belief in progress, in efficiency, in achievement and in rationality.

## Education and Democracy

The main research findings of Lipset (1960), have shown that the higher one's education, the more likely one is to believe in democratic values and support democratic practices. However, both Germany and Japan are examples of nations which had combined a high level of literacy with a totalitarian form of government. Particularly impressive is Lipset's evidence, that the working classes and the less educated tend to be more authoritarian in their attitudes and to be more likely to favour extremist political and religious groups. But, this tendency is not restricted only to working class. As Lipset himself has pointed out, 'data' from a number of countries demonstrate that classic Fascism is a movement of the propertied middle class. There is also some, although by no means conclusive evidence, that students in college become more liberated in their attitudes.

Thus, the influence of education upon political attitudes is much too complex. Although it may be argued, that high literacy rate is necessary for effective participation in a democratic government, there is no guarantee that Education and democratic attitudes are necessarily related.

**Education and Modernization**

Modernization is essentially a process, a movement from traditional or quasi-traditional order to certain desired types of technology and associated form of social structure, value orientation, motivations and norms. It is not simply a process of imitation, or just a superficial acquisition of certain traits and elements characteristic of the more advanced countries. Their selection in a logical order and sequence, and integration into the cultural pattern in a widely ramifying manner is essential. Thus, modernization involves the emergence of new behavioural system with certain distinctive characteristics, implying considerable value change (Dube, 1972).

Education can be a powerful instrument of modernization. Recent researches show that correlation between education and levels of national income, industrialization, urbanization, media exposure and participation in political and economic life are significant. To develop a climate of progress, attitude change is essential. Broadened mental horizon, one of the outcomes of education, permits absorption of new attitudes, on a larger scale. Also, as an instrument of instruction, education can directly teach many of the skills considered essential for the success of the programmes of modernization.

**Education and Value Change**

There is every indication that the educational system of Russia has transformed a largely illiterate and traditional oriented population into both a literate and industrialized work force. It has also managed to produce a generation which is, in the main, ideologically committed to the social order. The schools and colleges however, play only a minor role in the total process of indoctrination. Every agency of socialization is involved, such as the theatre, films, radio, TV, press, youth organizations etc., that is in striking contrast to most democratic systems, where the various media of socialization are only loosely controlled. Democratic societies are usually pluralistic and different, and even opposing system may be transmitted by different institutions. Thus, it would appear unreasonable to expect a school or educational system alone to achieve major changes in attitude. However, in his new classic study of 'Benington', Newcombe (1943), has shown that, given the right conditions, the experience of colleges and universities could change student's attitudes and values to a great extent.

**Conclusion**

The precise relationship of education to social, economic, political and cultural change can, therefore, be seen to be one of extreme complexity. The complexity is further aggravated by the fact that the educational institution is itself a part of the society which is changing. In essence, the aim of education in the present fast changing society should be to impart to the learner the life's know-how and to prepare him for change, copability, mobility, flexibility, uncertainties and emergencies.

No doubt, interplay between the sub-system of education and other sub systems, like economic, political and religious, regulate and promote social change considerably.

## References

Bowman, M.J. and Anderson, C.A., 'Concerning the role of Education in Development'; in Geertz, C. (ed.), *Old Societies and New States: The Quest for Modernity in Asia and Africa.* New York, Free Press, 1963, pp. 247-79.

Dare, R.P., *Education in Tokagava Japan,* London, Routledge and Kegan Paul, 1965, Ch. 10.

Durkheim, E., *Education and Sociology,* Free Press, Glencoe, 1956.

Durkheim, E., Suicide, Routledge, 1952.

Hoselitz, B.F., 'Investment in Education' in Coleman, J.S. (ed.), *Education and Political Development,* Princeton, Univ. Press, 1965, p. 522.

Huttington, E., 'World Power and Evolution', Yale Univ. Press, 1919; 'Civilization and Climate', Yale Univ. Press, 1924; 'Mainsprings of Civilization', Mentor Books, New American Library, 1959 in Ivor Morrish's 'Social Change and Education' in *The Sociology* of *Education,* London, George Allen and Unwin, 1952.

Lipset, S.M., *Political Man,* London, Heinemann, 1960.

MacIver, R.M. and Page, C.H., *Society: An Introductory Analysis,* Macmillan, 1950, Book III, 'Social Change'.

Mannheim, K., *Man and Society:* In an Age of Reconstruction, London, Roultedge, 1940.

Marx, Karl, *Capital,* Everyman Lib., Dent, 1930.

Morrish, Ivor, *The Sociology* of *Education: An Introduction,* London, George, Allen and Unwin, 1972.

Musgrave, P.W., *Technical Change, the Labour Force and Education,* Oxford, Pergamon Press, 1967, p. 262.

Newcombe, T.M., *Personality and Social Change: Attitude Formation in* a *Student Community,* New York, Dryden Press, 1943.

Ogburn, W.F. and Nimkoff, M.E., *A Handbook* of *Sociology,* London, Roultedge, 1947.

Sir Ronald Gould, *The Educational Implications* of *Social and Economic Change,* Opening Address: The Schools Council, 1967.

# 24

# Equalizing Educational Opportunity

The Indian society is materially poor, highly stratified and lacks vertical mobility. Having accepted democratic socialism as our political ideology, we have not been able to remove the glaring disparities based on education, income and traditional social status in our country. Instead of prioritizing and implementing various recommendations relating to equalization of educational opportunity the government is creating an illusion through the magic of reservation. This is, by and large, an attempt to make the caste system and other hierarchies as scape goats for its non-performance and failure to make the weak strong and strong just.

Infact, the government has been skilfully evading the basic issue of equalizing educational opportunities by instituting committees, organizing conferences and publishing policy reports on such marginal and superficial aspects of education like the 'school bag', 'action on action plan' and 'review of reviewed policy on education'. This is a sheer waste of time and of scarce resources of this poor country governed by the rich ministers and bureaucrats. Really speaking, our leaders have turned the whole nation into a 'talking parliament'. As a nation, we talk far better a game than to play it. A significant and basic difference would have been made to our educational system had the Ministry for Human Resource Development acted promptly and sincerely on the scheme of 'Operation Blackboard' recommended by the National Policy of Education (1986).

Indifference of the government to the egalitarian measures can be seen in the existing wide gap between per capita expenditure on rural and urban schools, and central and state universities. In the past 60 years, maldistribution of facilities, namely, for health, recreation and education has created marked educational disparities, regional imbalances and cultural disability in the country. "Our educational system" says Late J.D. Sethi, "is not merely iniquitous and dualistic but openly pitted against the poor". A major share of hard earnings of 80% under privileged is being spent on the education of the privileged 20%. Nearly, 30% of the Indian masses are living under the 'poverty line', but at the top of the pyramid of this system sits an extremely privileged minority controlling and appropriating most of the benefits of education for the upper and the elite classes. These socially indifferent and irresponsible superelites have "cradled at the top a distinctive style of popular bigotry".

The powerful group which controls the economic surplus and political power, has reduced education to the level of a 'purchasable commodity' by creating a snobbish and highly expensive parallel system of education, affordable only by the rich and affluent people. By using an alibi of 'resource crunch', the govt. is trying to shirk from its social obligation to finance higher education. Thus, the government has created space for allowing the politically powerful and financially dominant class to abuse the facility of higher education through the mechanism of privatism and free market. This official approach militates against the very concepts of a 'welfare state' and 'Social justice'. As we have seen in the last 15 years, this sort of unscrupulous neo-liberalization and privatization of education has further widened the divide between the 'class' and the 'mass', and the 'haves' and 'have-not' of education.

There is a vast scope for human effort to make-up the educational and cultural deficit caused by the poor home background and rigid social structure through the programmes of compensatory education. Keeping in view the specific needs of the socio-economically and culturally disadvantaged groups of learners, educational facilities of high quality must be made available to them. Simply chanting the mantra of "access to education for all" will not enable the deprived and depressed group of students to take advantage of the service of education, unless their parents are persuasively conscientised about the value of education, and barriers standing in the way of education of their wards are removed by practising positive discrimination and employing compensatory approaches. Those students who are at disadvantage due to their socio-economic and cultural deprivation can profit from educational institution if offered an enriched and smart educational setting with all necessary facilities under the healing and inspiring guidance of the best teachers trained specifically for the purpose. Utilization of the access to education available to such deprived learners would mostly depend upon removal of socio-economic and cultural disabilities from which they suffer. They also need an early momentum through a ' programme of early childhood care and education.

Equality has not yet become and enthusiastically pursued mission of all those who profess equality in education and other areas. Educational inquality due solely to history or poverty can be mitigated by implementing a time bound policy and programme of social justice focused on removing disabilities which do not permit the disadvantaged learners to profit from the educational arrangements available. No effort should be spared to ensure best facilities, including excellent teachers, for the education of deprived students from the primary stage of education. Periodic review and continuous monitoring is also necessary to see that quality education is delivered speedily to the wards of the socio-economically and culturally deprived people. Shirking from this responsibility will amount to depriving the country of contributions of a large human resource in terms of knowledge, skill and productivity. Equality of educational opportunity alone can not ameliorate the cultural and educational deficit of the disadvantaged students until they are enabled to achieve an equality of outcomes.

# 25

# Social Justice: Reconciling Equality With Excellence

It is generally believed that the concept of 'Social Justice' has a modern origin. However, people acquainted with Indian culture and tradition know it very well that some glympses of this idea can be traced back to the ancient Indian literature and ethics. The concept of equality had found its expression in almost all ancient and modern prayers. In these prayers and aphorisms, welfare of each and every individual is sought without discrimination. 'सर्वेषां मंगलं भवतु,' सर्वे 'भवन्तु सुखिनः' or 'आत्मवत् सर्व भूतेषु' are some of the examples that go to illustrate the Indian approach to equality and social justice. Stressing the value and importance of education and culture, the great law-giver Maharshi Manu also pronounced that every individual takes birth as a 'Shudra'. It is through 'Sanskar' or education, he or she acquires the status of a 'Dwij' (twice born) or a cultured and educated person ('जन्मना जायते शूद्रः संस्कारात् द्विज उच्चते'). Even today education is considered as a potent instrument of social equality and vertical mobility.

Social justice basically means playing fair to all the individual in the society. It seeks to give every one what is due to him or her, although it is not possible to determine what is due in absolute measure. The measures or parameters change with time, place and circumstance. Apart from just distribution of material goods and services of life, it also takes care of the reasonable requirements of body, mind and spirit. John Rawls (1971) in his theory of justice has advanced guiding principles to curb the rise of inequalities. He has introduced the 'principle of difference' which stands the conventional liberal and meritocratic notion of equality on its head. According to Rawls: "all social primary goods - liberty and opportunity, income and wealth, and the bases of self-respect - are to be distributed equally unless an unequal distribution of any or all of these goods is to the advantage of the least favoured". The aim of Rawls is to equalize not opportunity but results or outcomes. The logic of the present distribution of social goods and services which follows the principle of 'first come first served' may then be basically unfair. The Darwinist element in the liberal model appear to guide us to the wrong dimensions of inequality i.e. to those that can probably never be changed even by the most extreme forms of intervention (Tyler, 1977).

Social justice seeks to remove arbitrariness, discrimination and segregation in the official and social transactions through appropriate legal and constitutional remedies. The philosophy of social justice advocates protection and support by the state to the disadvantaged and deprived people through affirmative action or positive discrimination. In this age of ruthless competition in life and society, the state must come forward to extend adventitious aid to the underprivileged so that they may have the benefit of equal opportunity and its outcomes to facilitate their competition with the more advanced and privileged people in the race of life. Social justice is not aimed at pulling down the privileged sections of society. It simply prefers persuading and goading the 'haves' or 'well-to-do' people to make some sacrifice in the form of service to the 'have nots' of the depressed. No doubt, the process of uplifting the weaker section of the society should be facilitated without unreasonably and unduly affecting the interest and rights of the advantaged class. Peter must not be robbed to pay Paul. This action only prevents unjust enrichment and encouragement to a privileged few at the expense of large number of economically and culturally deprived masses.

The Indian society is caste ridden and tradition bound. It lacks openness and mobility. Violence, exploitation and dominance are almost inbuilt in the structure of this hierarchical society. This grim social reality pricked the conscience of those who were involved in the process of evolution of the Indian constitution. Through the supreme law of the land, they wanted to usher in a new social order based on political, economical and social justice. To make the idea of social justice realisable our constitution makers made fundamental freedom and fundamental rights an integral part of the constitution. The preamble of the constitution propounded the philosophy of social justice in the form of social values of justice, liberty, equality and fraternity. In point of fact, these four values are not mutually exclusive and they are the foundation of the constitution.

The scheme of social justice is presented and elaborated in part III, IV and XVI of the constitution and in other provisions thereof. The Indian constitution put an obligation on the state to promote the welfare of the people by securing and protecting effectively a social order in which social, economic and political justice shall inform all the institutions of national life. Besides, The 'Directives Principles of the State Policy', enshrined in the constitution, are potential rights and therefore, the constitution gives command to the State to create conditions for evolving them as enforceable rights.

In part IV (from article 34 to 51) of the constitution, the state is directed to make effective provisions for securing to its citizens, the right to work, to education, to public assistance in cases of unemployment, old age, sickness and disablement.

Similarly, the right to a living wage, to just and humane conditions of work, to decent standards of life and full employment of leisure and to social and cultural opportunities has been ensured. In article 45 the state is directed to provide free and compulsory education for all the children until they complete the age of fourteen years. Apart from that, the state is also directed generally to raise the level of nutrition and standard of living of its people and to improve public health, to organise agriculture and animal husbandry, to promote the educational and economic interests of scheduled castes, scheduled tribes and other weaker sections of the society.

The concept of equality is central to the philosophy of social justice. It is argued that although human beings are not created equal in all respects, yet they should be treated equally in all respects. But equal opportunity can not be given without giving consideration to special ability, talent and creativity of individuals. Aristotle was justified in saying the "it is no more just to treat unequals equally than to treat equals unequally" The idea of equality is neither an identical appreciation of talent and ability, nor a uniformity of treatment under all circumstances. It is certainly an equality of rights. The notion of fundamental equality propels us towards a position maintaining that all humans be treated alike unless there is a sufficient reason for treating them differently. An agreed upon criteria could be that the educational treatment accorded to each person should be in accordance with his or her unique needs, abilities and circumstances, and also according to the degree of difference exhibited by the ability, aptitude, need and circumstances of the individual. By following the criteria of discrimination, we do not accord greater equality of treatment, but we rather respect inequalities, and at the same time feel free to alter the criteria for discrimination. We should also take steps to eliminate the inequalities which are unjust, disproportionate and inappropriate.

It is clear that equality as a value is in no way absolute and that it must take its place among other competing values when we are decoding educational policy. Therefore, it is important to attempt to gauge the widest possible range of consequences of a policy based on the goal of equality of opportunity. Usually we increase competition, and we may or may not judge the consequence to be desirable. It is very necessary to estimate and analyse the individual and social consequences of competition, because ruthless competition has the potential of threatening fraternal feelings, unity and ease of communication. In a society like India, and some other eastern and western society, where stratification is recognized and accepted, there may be strong ties and feelings of security.

"When a society gives up hereditary stratification," says John W. Gardner, "There are two ways in which it may deal with the dramatic individual differences in ability and performance that emerge. One way is to limit or work against individual differences, protecting the slow learners and curbing the swift. This is the path of equalitarianism. The other way is simply to 'let the best man win.' As we shall see, in their moderate forms each of these points of view - equalitarianism and competitive performance - is a necessary ingredient of a healthy society. We shall also note that each point of view can be carried to harmful extremes." Extreme emphasis on competitive achievement or performance will lead to 'raw striving' resulting in to neglect, and brutal treatment of the less able or less vigorous or less aggressive. Gardner further points out that such ill treatment 'may wantonly injure those whose temperament or whose values make them unwilling to engage in performance rivalries; it may penalize those whose undeniable excellences do not add up to the kind of performance that society at any given moment chooses to reward. Therefore, the basic question is how to, reconcile the two poles of equality and excellence without harming the able or the talented, and without hurting the dignity of the less able or less pushing.

Answer to this question lies in helping the less able by subsidizing their education, and the able by providing enrichment and acceleration in their pursuit of studies. So far, researches have revealed that talent is multi dimentional and, with the exception of some mentally damaged individuals, every body is talented. What is primarily needed is greater investment of resources for the development and nurturance of talent of those who are placed in the adverse socio-economic circumstances by the accident of birth. By and large, we remain one of the most brutal societies of the world where accident of birth and not worth still decides the destiny.

The concept of equality of opportunity is not as simple as it sounds. Inequality is multi-causal. It can not be explained away by a single determinant, however strong its influence on education might be. In the debates on educational inequality the educational system itself has been very often singled out to be the cause of inequality. There are other educational sociologists like Christopher Jencks (1972) and James Coleman (1966) who attribute educational inequality to deficient home or family background of the learner, and therefore they think that the educational system matters the least.

On the basis of causes of inequality in education discovered by different researches educational inequalities have been classified as follows. The **first** kind of inequality is that of 'achievement' in different school subjects. The **second** refers to inequality in educational 'background', usually in the family or home. The **third** inequality is that of 'aptitude or ability', that is, of potential for learning. The **fourth** type of inequality is that of 'school environment'. The **fifth** inequality is connected with tangible 'outcomes' of education or examination results. The final or **sixth** inequality is termed as 'life chances' which is associated with the status and income of the individual. These are, to a large extent influenced by the type, quality and duration of schooling one has received.

The distribution of all the six dimensions of educational inequality presented above appears to be isomorphous with the distribution of most of other 'goods' of power, wealth and services, whether individually or institutionally defined. In this context, the 'difference principle' of Rawls theory of justice is very valuable and relevant. It has two aspects of relevance to policy. The main one is the 'principle of redress' for individuals who are disadvantaged. Rawls' suggests that greater resources might be spent on the education of the less rather than the more intelligent and able, at least, during the earlier years of school. This is similar to a 'compensatory model' but it is derived from a principle of fairness that sees education as 'good' in its own right, not as an instrument of social-engineering. The underprivileged and poor have a right to more education because they have less of everything. The second implication for social policy is that talents are to be defined as a common asset. All are to share equally (or unequally in the positive discrimination sense) its fruits. Equality of opportunity should produce equal benefits both social and individual.

"Policy makers lose patience with sociologists", says Tyler (1977), "Who tell them that inequality is rooted in their middle-class attitudes and ideologies, or that the only thing that will improve the educational chances of the poor is political revolution. The problems of illiteracy, material and social deprivation cannot be solved by decree. In liberal democratic society, there are questions of justice and equity that must be remedied in the terms of the given situation."

The challenge for school, college and university is to nurture the differences among students in such a way that instead of promoting exclusiveness, the differences serve to enhance unity. Just as the differences in a good orchestra enhance the unity of music. Thus, a kind of equality is achieved where each student is equally free to be himself or herself and to explore his uniqueness, but all are bound together by feelings of respect, interdependence and indispensability (Nash,

1993)..This is the sure way to reconcile equality with excellence. John Rawls has sounded appropriate caution in his remark that justice should not be confused with an all-inclusive vision of a good society, it is only a part of such conception. But there is also much substance in Martin Luther King's (Jr) assertion that "injustice anywhere is a threat to justice everywhere."

## References

Coleman, James S. *et al*. (1966) *Report on Equality of Educational Opportunity*. US Govt. Printing office for Department of Health, Education and Welfare, 26.

Jencks, Christopher *et al*. (1972) *Inequality : A Reassessment of the Effect of Family and Schooling in America*. New York : Basic Books.

Rawls, John (1971) A Theory of Justice. Oxford: Clarendon Press.

Tyler, William (1977) *The Sociology of Educational Inequality*. London: Methuen & Co. Ltd.

# 26

# Human Rights Education: Need and Nature

Indian tradition is predominantly a Hindu tradition. In ancient India Hindu Dharma was known as only 'Dharma' or 'Sanatan Dharma' which embodied the attributes of antiquity, eternity, time - testedness and humanitarianism. In other words, it was based on eternal human, social and spiritual values. Manu, the great law-giver, also defined Dharma in terms of ten basic values, namely: *Dhriti, Kshama, Dam, Astey, Shauch, Indriy-nigraha, Buddhi, Vidya, Satya* and *Akrodh.* Vyas, the guru of gurus, putforth the essence of eighteen *Puranas* by saying : 'परोपकाराय पुण्यः पापाय परपीड़नम'. Besides emphasizing universal brotherhood it insisted on cooperative, non-exploitative and mutually nurturing relationship with the nature, animal-world and inanimate objects. All ancient Hindu prayers aim at the welfare, prosperity and peace for all irrespective of race, religion and nation. An enormous feeling of respect for every object and particle of the earth was cultivated and transmitted from generation to generation. This attitude is condensed in one of the verses of the *Rigveda* in which it is highlighted that the earth is the mother and we are her sons and daughters. भूमिः माता पुत्रोहं प्रथिव्याः Special consideration was given to inculcate and promote a liberal outlook in the children, youth and adults through discourses and dialogues.

Large heatedness was fostered and small mindedness was discouraged. This is summed up in the aphorism: अयं निजः परोवेति गणना लघुचेतसाम् उदार चरितानाम् तु वसुधैव कुटुंबकम्. It is also ordained in the Yajurveda that in this world one man is a protector of the other : मनुष्यां मनुष्यं परिपातु विश्वतः, and here in India the whole world is transformed in to a human nest: 'यत्र भवति विश्व एक नीड़म्।

The renowned philosopher and an eminent historian Arnold Toynbee took note of this is all embracing humanism of Indian culture and observed that: "at this supremely dangerous moment in human history, the only way of salvation for mankind is an Indian way. Here we have the attitude and the spirit that can make it possible for human race to grow together into a single family and in this atomic age this is the only alternative to destroying our selves." Similarly, comparing the Indian approach and attitude with that which permeates the culture and civilization of other countries, A.L. Basham (1954) maintained that "........overall impression is that in no other part of the ancient world were the relations of man and man, and man and the state, so fair and humane. In no other civilization were slaves so few in numbers and in no other ancient law book are their rights so well protected as in *Arthashastra.* No other ancient law giver proclaimed such noble ideals of fair play in battle as did Manu to us. The most striking feature of ancient Indian civilizations is humanity".

In the *Manu Smiriti,* Manu had laid down the relative importance of five virtues (Wealth, Brother, Age, Action and Vidya). In Shlok no. 112 he had made it very explicit that a Shudra of ninety years would be worthy of respect and honour if he had attained higher standard on the stated scale of virtues. "And I have seen," Says Swami Vivekanand, "Mehtar Tyagis in the forest of Hrishikesh wearing the garb of the sannyasin, studying the Vedanta and many a proud high-class men would be glad to sit at their feet and learn. And why not? अन्यादपि परम धर्मम् (Supreme knowledge can be learnt even from the man of low birth.")

Thus, it is very clear that we have a long tradition and culture of egalitarianism and reverence for each and every particle of the earth and the universe. The concept and idea of human right was inherent in our thought and culture. The ancient legacy is conducive to the present day movement for creating human rights consciousness in the masses. The philosophy of immanence of god (ईशावास्यं इदं सर्वम्), transmigration of soul and man as a potential God has given much philip and credence to the uniqueness, unity and dignity of human beings.

In the true Indian way of life, simple living and high thinking were also considered a prerequisite for removing disparity in the realm of wealth, health and quality of life. Mahatma Gandhi exemplified and reemphasized this style of life along with non-violence and non-acquisitiveness. On the other hand, the Western life style based on limitless individualism, affluence and consumption, in the words of Mathew Arnold, is "materializing the upper class, vulgarizing the middle class and brutalizing the lower class". This type of subservience of Western societies to machine and material is creating great divide between nations and civilizations contributing to the phenomenon of marginalization and exclusion. Does this approach to living and progress not prove that the Western concern and claim for human rights are hallow and propagandist?

## Need for Human Rights Awareness

Although men and women are perceived as crowning excellence of the creation, and they are also considered as measure of all things; yet in the modem times the political, economic and technological forces in tandem with market fundamentalism and globalization are militating against almost all the human and spiritual feelings and tendencies of man. "Like social Darwinism, market fundamentalism tends to disregard altruism and cooperation. According to George Soros, the world capital markets function in an amoral dimension and that is okay. But when the same rules come to govern all the rest of social and economic life, then civilization itself is endangered". Infact, civilization is an .act of civility, which is meant for freedom, creativeness, love, reason and relatedness. But, the abnormal and unprecedented pressure and insistence of Western thinking on developing one dimensional 'economic man' is tending to divest man of his other dimensions. Econocentrism and technocentrism are prompting man to 'get rich quick by throwing others into the ditch'. What is essential today is to look at the man as a whole in all his manifestations and dimensions. The human rights efforts must be, therefore, directed to resist and prevent all those attempts and policies which are aiming at 'thingification' of human beings, or reducing them to mere objects and instruments of the system.

"Notwithstanding the vast array of international regional measures", says K.P. Saxena, "gross violation of human rights are widely rampant. In many parts of the world observance of and respect for civil and political rights are conspicuous by their absence. Arbitrary arrest, long term detention without trial, political disappearance, and abuse of psychiatry for political ends are widely rampant. The prerequisites for enjoyment of civil and political rights, i.e., rule of law and democratic system of government have been ignored with impunity. One man, one party, military dictatorship and other kind of dictatorial regimes characterize a larger part of the world" .

The need for human rights education has been justified in the Universal Declaration of Human Rights (1948) and in similar other documents and covenants. Any education, worth its name is basically concerned with the process of bringing out the innate capacities of the learner. There is also another complementary process of socialization which is concerned with bringing up the child and the youth. Socialization aims at initiating the young generation in the norms, values and belief system of the community and the larger society. This process, in no case, should remain confined to the mores and values of the culture of the dominant class. In other world, the process of socialization inducts the child in the culture of the society and the nation. The agencies of education and socialization support and reinforce the culture by making the children and the youth comprehend and critically examine various aspects, namely: social, economic, political, scientific, technological and religious. Looking to the unprecedented importance and power allowed to and enjoyed by the political system, the process of 'political socialization' has acquired greater priority and importance today than in the earlier times. Therefore, acquaintance with and understanding of the democratic institutions, democratic values enshrined in the preamble of the constitution, provisions of fundamental rights, freedoms, duties and directive principles of State policy made in the Indian constitution, have become all the more necessary and urgent. Human rights educators are required to focus their attention on this aspect of political socialization, which is important part of human rights.

**Nature of Human Rights Education**

Thoreau, who was a source of inspiration for Mahatma Gandhi, was an ardent advocate of human rights. He was of the view that human rights be given to the human beings as gifts. There are other thinkers who wish to grant the privilege of human rights to men and woman in return of their duties. But the best course would be to strike a balance between these two standpoints. Rights and duties are the two sides of the same coin of human development and social progress. Since human beings are self directing and have a sense of accountability to the society, it should be left to themselves to blend rights and duties in a manner which is befitting of a human being. On the other hand, there is a symbiotic relationship between human beings and the plants and the animal world. Hence, plants and animals also need a considerable degree of safety and protection from men's cruelty and barbarism. Even inanimate substances like air, water and food grains also require a guarantee and immunity from the human acts of pollution and manipulation. It would be, therefore, in the interest of the human beings to grant, preserve and protect such privileges for non-human part of the universe and biosphere. While talking loudly about human rights education we can afford to ignore animal and plant rights at our own peril. It is heartening to recall that such unwritten rights and freedoms for plants and animals were an integral part of human life before the onslaught of unreasonable greed and materialism in the present times.

The human rights education is an individual and group endeavor to create a universal culture of human rights. To accomplish this objective, relevant knowledge and skills are imparted and attitudes are modified at every level of formal and informal learning. This kind of education is general and liberal in its nature. Its curriculum is very wide and comprehensive and embraces almost all branches of knowledge which have individual, social and ecological consequences. It places its emphasis on recognition of, respect for and realization of the human rights in terms of preservation of dignity and solidarity of human beings to ultimately accomplish human and social development in harmony with nature. In the philosophy and principles of human rights education, there is no place for struggle for existence, survival of the fittest and dialecticism. It is based on the core concept of autonomy of individual unfoldment with social consideration. Hence, human rights education proceeds in an atmosphere of interdependence, cooperation and mutuality. The clients and consumers of this education are enabled to understand, accommodate and appreciate the differences in individuals and sub cultures. They are encouraged to focus their attention on the 'commonalities' which are the building blocks of emotional, national and international understanding. Through conversation and dialogue the qualities of democratic attitude, scientific spirit and philosophic tolerance are inculcated. Since the nations and the world are full of diversities and pluralistic characteristics, it is considered desirable and beneficial to direct the efforts of human rights educators towards developing enlightened 'multiple loyalties' in place of sectarian or one dimensional affinity to a single caste, creed, race, religion of culture. Human rights education can be conceived, in the words of Will Durant: "a delightful and ennobling intimacy with the cultural heritage of mankind."

A large part of the world and our own country consist of culturally deprived and economically disadvantaged masses. Human rights education has the responsibility to make the week people strong and strong people just, so that the women, handicapped and destitutes don't feel excluded or marginalized. On account of the forces of domination and exploitation, the poor masses have been deprived of all good things of life. They have also been disabled to participate in decision making and to protest against injustice due to lack of information and education. As a result of living in humanly intolerable and degrading condition of life, they have been dehumanized to the extent that they prefer to escape freedom and dialogue. They have, therefore, accepted destitution as their destiny. Human rights education has an important role to awaken life and response in this fossilized human-mass through the programmes of conscientization and empowerment by restoring to them the right to information and to development. In Amartya Sen's words: "development is freedom". Therefore, a synthesis of civil liberties model and the basic concepts of development would be an appropriate approach to social and economic advancement for the disadvantaged people. John Stuart Mill was right in his remark that "liberty meant each person's right to think for himself or herself to follow his or her intellect to whatever conclusion it may lead in an atmosphere that forbade mental slavery". Thus, human rights education is both liberating and developmental.

In conclusion, it would be relevant to say that a human being should be viewed in totality and harmony of all the major dimensions of his or her personality. This holistic approach is the core and crux of any programme of human rights education. Human rights education forms the part and parcel of every subject or discipline taught in the educational institutions in formal and non-formal setting. It is infact a 'Commonwealth' of all the areas of studies. Success of such a programme depends to a great extent on the way the teachers transact the curriculum and intervene in the student-teacher interaction. The outcomes of human rights education programme hinges on the manner and quality of treatment the teacher gives to the subject matter. For the effectiveness of this programme an anthropological, interactive and dialogical approach is essential.

Human rights education is not the substitution of any form or stage of education, but the integration of all forms and residences of education into a more comprehensive and unified view of learning and its relationship to human action and aspiration. It is therefore not only a collective concept for the various branches of educational studies, but also an area of research with its own scientific sets of questions. The whole concept and methodology of human rights education can be compressed in the following Hippy Slogan of Sixties: "I am the human being: Don't fold, spindle or mutilate".

# 27

# Peace Education: Beating Swords into Plowshares

In the eighteenth century, Voltaire wanted to know the steps by which men passed from barbarism to civilization. In my opinion, perhaps, the major step taken by men, in this respect, was to accept the value of peace and harmony in the society to promote 'cultural creation' or civilization. Infact, civilization begins where chaos and insecurity end. "For when fear is overcome" says Will Durant (1954), curiosity and constructiveness are free, and man passes by natural impulse towards understanding and embellishment of life". Although, barbarism does not appear in that primitive ferocious form in the modern times, yet it continues to inflict the humanity through deprivation, discrimination, segregation, domination and violation of human rights.

Man differs from the beast only by education. Through civilizing influence of various socializing and educating institutions, greed is transmuted into thrift, violence into argument, murder into litigation and suicide into philosophy (Durant, 1954). Thus, man's propensity for violence can be transformed into non-violent disposition leading to the rule of law, order, peace and compassion in the society. To have a peaceful, affectionate and sane society, we must strive to create a culture of non-violence in all organizations and institutions. Non-violence is a power which can be enjoyed equally by all - rich and poor and Weak and strong. Literature on non-violence suggests that the concept of non-violence has at least eight components: peace, equality, fearlessness, humility, love, self-control, truth and tolerance. Of course, these components are not exclusive of each other, and peace appears to be a major part of non-violence.

Peace is a vital part of our collective consciousness. It is an attitude towards life which, by restraining violence, strengthen social cohesion and makes the life worthliving. Peace is not a thing that we can achieve at some point and neglect it thereafter. As a matter of fact, peace today has come to be treated as a pre-condition of survival, growth and development. The way to peace is not through weakness. "We do not fight violence" says Mahatma Gandhi,"so much as weakness. Nothing is worthwhile unless it is strong. Neither good nor evil. Absolute evil is better than emasculated goodness. Moaning pacifism is the death-knell of peace; it is cowardice and lack of faith. Let those who do not believe, who fear, withdraw! The way to peace leads through self-sacrifice" (In Romain Rolland, 1924). India has been sticking to this unique faith in peace since ancient times. Even today prayers and recitations for making peace are made during different social and religious ceremonies. The science and art of peace will be of great importance in any future-oriented solution to the problems of our time. Real happiness and prosperity can only be achieved through peace education, since peace education helps the individual to reach more mature decision regarding his responsibilities as a world citizen.

Peace education is a form of education that goes to its own unalterable human presupposition. If human beings are to become fundamentally ready for, capable of and skilled in the peace making effort of an epoch of world peace which is yet to be secured, they must be prepared for this situation by peace education. Put differently, peace education connotes a generalized approach to education for global responsibility in a planetary nuclear age. It operates at all levels and in all spheres of learning, includes all fields of relevant knowledge and is life long, continuous process (Reardon, 1988).

Peace education of this type has primarily to develop readiness, capability and skills for peace. Readiness for peace includes the possibility of recognizing conflict as much and seeking a resolution in such a manner that the basis of co-operation is consolidated. The relevant capabilities for peace are the human qualities needed to shape peace as a social process appropriate to the circumstances. Finally, peace skills include not only those of recognizing conflict and acting co-operatively but also an intelligent openness for involvement in peace in one's own sphere, combined with a sense of responsibility for supra-regional and supra-national concerns (Rohrs, 1992).

Peace is an ontological principle concerning the humanizing of the human beings as much as interpersonal and international relations. Positive peace has become the concept connoting a world in which the structural violence has been significantly reduced, if not eliminated. The fundamental virtue of peace is justice. Both justice and peace can be seen as two sides of the same coin. Therefore, peace can not be achieved simply by restrictive measures to exclude violence, conflict and war. Negative peace, in the sense of a formal ordering power, is a caricature of real peace. Peace is individual. It concerns the whole person and his way of life, which must ensure the conditions for freedom, justice and happiness.

Peace education is not a special subject. Principles of peace-education can permeate all educational and teaching content. Every subject, from Anthropology to Zoology, can be guided by peace-education in that its point of view may be didactically emphasized. Generally the whole of school and college life must be influenced by the spirit of peace education. Peace education must primarily be experienced rather than taught if it is to significantly affect the young people and direct them towards the creation of peace. Peace education seeks to develop a critical awareness of world problems and a global perspective on their resolution. In essence, peace education promotes and strengthen a peaceful way of thinking and acting. It is a contemporary effort to "beat swords into plowshares". It is an attempt to transfer technical skills, machinery and capital, currently committed to war preparation, to the production of socially useful items (Cassidy, 1987).

What serves the purpose of understanding and co-operation across international borders is included in peace education. 1n this sense, international education corresponds to peace education. Some educationists feel that peace education is more comprehensive than education for internationalism. The goal of peace education is to create individual capable of critical thinking having feeling of solidarity and empathy with the less privileged. He is a person who, on the basis of his or her own conviction and humanistic orientation towards life, is able to act in cooperation with others to create a more just world.

Some of the more important topics to be treated by peace-education are the following :-

(1) The East-West polarity and its nuclear threat to human life;

(2) The North-South conflict and its international vertical division of labour resulting in extensive poverty in the southern hemisphere;

(3) Pollution and the destruction of the environment;

(4) The scarcity of food and resources;

(5) The population explosion;

(6) The problem of broadening understanding for human rights, and social justice (Wulf, 1974).

A long and hard examination of the above mentioned

issues is needed leading to a decrease in prejudices and in thinking of the enemy in terms of stereotypes. It implies a change in self-awareness contributing to a deepened understanding of society and the world.

As is the case with all education, peace education should take place in three areas: knowledge, skill/action and attitude. Together these areas constitute an integral whole. Peace education can not be neutral or value-free. It is essential to have the courage to work on the basis of moral humanistic values. Success of peace education efforts greatly depend on the amount of co-operation mobilized between the field of education, peace-related research and practical politics.

## References

Durant, Will (1954). *The Story of Civilization : Part I Our Oriental Heritage.* N.Y., Simon and Schuster.

Cassidy, K.J. (1987). "Beating Swords into Plowshares From Military Spending to Economic Conversion". In Hermann Rohrs, "Securing Lasting World Peace through Education". *Education*,Vol. 45, 1992.

Reardon, Betty A.(1985). *Global Responsibility*. N.Y.: Teachers Collage Press.

Rohrs, Hermann (1992). Securing lasting World Peace through Peace Education, *Education* 45, 1-17.

Rolland, Romain (1924). *Mahatma Gandhi: The Man who became one with the Universal being.* New Delhi: Publication Division, Ministry of I & B, Govt. of India.

Wulf ch(ed.) (1574) *Handbook of Peace Education*. International Peace Association, Frankfurt/Oslo.

# 28

# Research in Social Sciences : Overcoming Phobia for Subjectivity

Research is not a ritual of accumulating a large amount of knowledge and keeping it in the cold storage of the library for its application in the future. It is an attitude of mind focused on the knowability and explorability of the world. It is questioning or an inquisitive mind-set which throws doubt on the utility of existing knowledge and traditional skills. Research is a quest for new knowledge, novel ideas and innovative practices. It raises questions and answers them. It identifies, problems and attempts to find out the solutions. It is a process of continuous scrutiny, evaluation and renewal. In the time of change, knowledge will grow incroasingly perishable. An obvious idea of today is often yesterday's discovery. Today's facts are tomorrow's outdated information, and who knows yesterday's myth may become tomorrow's reality. Hence, research, as a process, must engage itself in continuous renewal of knowledge and ideas. In the days of rapid change, it is expressly desirable to overcome obsolescence and inertness of knowledge and ideas by subjecting them to careful review and research.

No one can seriously deny that none of our social problems are capable of wise resolution without formulation of its contents by an expert mind. To formulate rightly the nature of social problem is far more difficult than to formulate rightly a problem in physics or chemistry. In social matters, where the problem of measurement is infinitely more difficult, the expert is entitled to far less assurance. It is equally difficult to arrive at a right interpretation of an answer found for a fundamental social question.

In the report of the *Gulbenkian Commission* (1997) on the restructuring of the social sciences, social science has been defined as "an enterprise of the modern world. Its root lies in the attempt, full blown since the sixteenth century, and part and parcel of the construction of our modern world, to develop systematic secular knowledge about reality that is some how validated empirically".

In this context it is relevant to go through the definition of Sociology presented by the renowned sociologist Late Prof. M. N. Sriniwas in his book: *Indian Society through Personal Writings* (1998). Sriniwas says that "Sociology is a science in the sense that it studies human societies in space and time in a systematic and comparative manner, but it is also an art in the sense that it is much more than information and knowledge about societies. It strives to achieve understanding, and this is impossible without imagination and empathy. In some areas social knowledge involves not only the intellect but the emotions, not only the head but the heart". For that matter, it is a novel and different viewpoint from almost all other ideas put forth so far, by many sociologists for defining the science of society.

From the sociological point of view, research is most important tool for advancing knowledge, promoting progress and enabling man to relate more effectively to his environment to accomplish his purposes and to resolve his conflicts. It is oriented towards the discovery and study of the relationships that exist among the phenomena of the world in which we live and interact.

In social science research, because of the complexity of the variables under consideration, "exception are more frequent", says George J. Mouly (1964), "and are often more drastic and damaging. In fact, the many exceptions to the generalizations of the social sciences have led some people to question whether a human science is possible. The point is frequently made that human behavior is not subject to scientific determination and control, that because man is possessed of a free will and is capable of choice, he operates independently of the forces surrounding him."

**Subjectivity**

Subjectivity has been defined most often as the importation of the biases of the researcher into the collection and interpretation of the data. This is seen as distorting the data, and therefore of reducing its validity. But, it is also said that what is thought to be 'subjective knowledge' is merely the knowledge of those who are socially powerful and occupy positions of power. Therefore, the Report of the *Gulbenkin Commission on the Restructuring of the social sciences (Wallerstein et. al., 1997)* observes that what is needed to be guarded against is that social science does not get reduced to a "miscellaney of private views". We should not write history in the name of existing power structures and the intellectual activity be freed from disabling external pressures and from mythology and revealed and/or accepted wisdom or ideology.

Attempts are on to liberate the human thought still further. The idea of the 'neutral scientist' advanced by the positivist social scientists has been proved futile and ineffective to free scholarship from arbitrary orthodoxy since "no scientist can ever be extracted from his or her social context. Every measurement changes reality in the attempt to record it. Every conceptualization is based on philosophical commitments. In time, the widespread belief in fictive neutrality has become in itself a major obstacle to increasing the truth value of our findings. If this poses a great problem for the natural scientists, it is an even greater problem for the social scientists" (W allerstein, *et. al.*, 1997).

"What I am trying to say", remarks Fred N. Kerlinger (1 978), "is that strong subjective involvement is a powerful motivation for acquiring an objective approach to learn much about science, research design and research methods without considerable personal involvement". Thus, Kerlinger pleads that the students be encouraged to discuss, argue, debate and even fight about research. They should take a stand and be opinionated. Later they should try to soften the opinionation into intelligent conviction and controlled emotional commitment. Similar opinion has been expressed by the former Supreme Court Judge of the US, Justice Arthur Goldberg. He says: "we can not be impartial. We can only be intellectually honest, that is, aware of our passions, on guard against them and prepared to warn our readers of the dangers into which our partial views may lead them. Impartiality is our dream and honesty a duty."

It is worth reverting to Prof. Shriniwas's book *Indian Society through Personal Writings* (1998). The 'Introduction' of this book presents a persuasive argument for engaging research in the area of biographies and autobiographies. Such writings not only focus on the lives of particular individuals, but they also shed light on the cultural and social milieu of the subjects. Some novels also achieve this in a remarkable way. According to Shriniwas, the insights they provide are usually beyond the reach of sociological study. He felt unhappy to find that biographies, autobiography and novels are not made use of in sensitizing sociologists to cultures other than their own. It may be so because of the reason they believe their discipline claims to be a science, and therefore, it needs quantitative data, not the symbolic representation and qualitative analysis suitable for literary and historical investigations. Due to this erroneous belief, scholars and researchers working in the areas of social sciences are mostly given training in statistics and quantitative analysis of research studies. Sriniwas complains that "no attempt is made to train the student to be a sensitive observer, to watch out for changes in moods, and in the body language of the observed".

Another lacuna that Sriniwas highlighted was the preoccupation of the sociologists with the study of one or other part of their own culture and society. They have not yet tried to use their own lives as ethnographic data for analysis, "The hazards in the use of such material", he says, "are only too well-known. There is a desire to present oneself as a much nicer person than one is, and exaggerate one's achievements and deprecate or ignore the achievements of others, and so on. The temptation to exhibitionism, tear one's hair and beat one's breasts in public, can not also be ignored, even though it is much less likely than the possibility mentioned earlier. The central theme in an anthropological autobiography should be the subject's progress through shifting cultural milieus which means that the light the narrative sheds on cultural and social changes, has to be incidental".

Sriniwas pleads that the movement from studying one's own culture or a niche in it, to studying oneself as an ethnographic field, is a natural one. In the West, he observes, anthropology started as a study of 'the other' generally a weaker, inferior and exploited 'other'. But in India it has largely been a study of the 'self' or the 'self-in-the other'. No doubt, this should extend to include one's own life. Thus, "Sociology of the self should be a rich field for research, given the diversities and unities, inherited by the members of the Indian civilization. There is also a need for studies on the relationship of culture and technology.

In the 21st century technology has become the rage of the age. Lest it takes the form of 'technopoly' and starts usurping the cultural space, steps should be taken to make in-depth study of the relationship between technology and culture in the Indian society. The number of people having an ear for music, an eye for a good painting and an inclination for literature is decreasing day by day. A tendency of taking drugs, indulging in coercive and unnatural sex, and resorting to violence on slightest provocation is on the rise. Thus, the balance between technology and culture is being disturbed at the detriment of the larger society.

Now, at the global level it is being increasingly realized that there is an implicit contract between big business and society, or indeed between whole economic sectors and society. A new idiom of 'corporate responsibility' has gained currency, since the day fraudulent behaviour of Enron and Tyco has come to public notice. In the past few years some of the accountancy firms and technology companies have started employing social anthropologists or 'people watchers' to study and analyse the behaviour of the employees. This shift also reflects the growing complexity of public and private sector 'work-places' and the realization by companies and governments that they must operate in a global environment. In America, anthropologists have been hired by technological groups including Intel, Microsoft, Apple and Xerox. In the UK the 'people watchers' can be found not just pacing in the corridors of blue-chip companies but also the Ministry of Defence, the National Health Service and the Foreign Office, as well as non-governmental aid agencies (Gillian Tett, 2005).

Simon Roberts of Edinburgh University investigated, in 1990, the impact of satellite TV in Varanasi, and showed how TV shows affected households and how they looked on the world. Intel anthropologists spend much of their time "out in the field", living at close quarters in households around the world to analyse the way they use technology. Perhaps the most eye-catching project has been a three-year study of how technology is used by Asia's fast-growing middle class. The anthropologists found Chinese families who take their mobile phones to temples to be blessed or burn paper cell phones in funeral rituals, and Muslim devotees who use the GPS on their phone to locate Mecca for prayers.

Anne Kirah, a senior design anthropologist at Microsoft, is roaming the world to see how families use technology such as Windows. She is working like a trend-hunter. She goes into people's homes and watch them from dawn to dusk with fresh, neutral eyes to spot and understand cultural patterns. She thinks of herself as an advocate for the consumers, helping to get products they want designed. The social anthropologists in various technological companies, thus, try to understand the cultural context in which technology is used around the world. They try to understand how technology is being used in family groups as tools to assert power, negotiate relationships, mark rites of passage or in social bonding.

"The desire of social scientists to do some thing about the dreadful state of the social world", observed Dr. Jagjeet Singh (1980), "is laudable. But the methods of natural science they employ has not worked in the anticipated way. Whatever the problem to which it has been applied - whether urban riots, inflation, unemployment, drunkenness, dope, racial strife, city slums, social inequality, rural backwardness or what have you - it has left open every question about what to do to solve the problems. It has not yet yielded the solutions sought for the simple reason that the key to the many problems of mankind is not in the area it can illumine. It is in an area of darkness the social scientists dare not explore because there is no light over there. They are somewhat like the noctural drunk, who on his way back home drops the key to his apartment near a bush, but comes to look for it under a lamp post, because there is no light under the bush".

## References

Kerlinger, Fred N. (1978). *Foundations of Behavioural Research* (Second Edition). Delhi: Smurjeet Publications.

Mouley, George, J. (1964). *The Science of Educational Research.* Delhi: Eurasia Publishing House.

Singh, Jagjeet (1980). Failure of Grand Science. *Hindustan Times,* May 15.

Sriniwas, M.N. (1998). *Indian Society through Personal Writings.* Delhi: Oxford University Press.

Tett, Gillian (2005). Lost Tribes of Acme Accounting. *Financial Times,* May 21-22.

Wallerstein, Immanuel *et.al.* (1997). *Open the Social Sciences,* (Report of the Gulbenkian Commission on the Restructuring of the Social Sciences). New Delhi: Vistar Publications.

# 29

# Revolutionizing Teaching and Learning of Science

To keep pace with the progression of science, a change in the approach and technique of imparting science education was identifiable in the countries of the west in the nineteen thirtees. It began to gather momentum just after the World War two. Then, an unprecedented eruption of activity in the teaching and learning of science was witnessed. In the year 1957, when the Russian 'Sputnik' was known to the world, the concern about science-education was increasingly intensified.

The National Science Foundation and other private trust in the U.S.A. initiated a number of curricular reforms leading to a drastic review and revision of text and instructional materials. These were completed in early sixtees. Continuation of efforts in U.K. was a generous grant by Nuffield Foundation to embark upon an ambitions science teaching project. The Organization for European Economic Development stated in 1963 : "We believe that it is necessary to change completely the content of school physics courses, the attitude of the mind of the science teacher towards his aim and purpose which the teaching of physics is considered to fulfill. Nothing less than a radical change will suffice." Infact, this radical approach is very much needed today, in our country, to revolutionise science-education.

In the post-independence period our national attitude towards science underwent a great change. The need for a pervasive change in the system of science education from the school to the higher education was keenly felt. In the distant past, organizations like U.G.C. and N.C.E.R.T. had, more than once, emphasized the need for a coordinated plan of action for an overall improvement of science-education. These bodies also reiterated desirability of partnership between the college and school teachers in this direction. By organizing 'Summer Institutes', steps were taken in 1960s and 70's to upgrade contents, teaching and learning of science. Later on, somehow, inertia crept in and therefore nationwide attempts were not made to transform science-education.

Due to indifference and inaction of agencies and organizations, responsible for maintaining standards of science education, teaching and learning of science in schools and colleges went on deteriorating to the extent that the scientific advisor to the govt. of India has to sound a wake-up call for all those people who are associated with science education and research, to expedite their efforts for improving teaching and learning of science to prevent its degeneration into a dogma. Most recently' the National Knowledge Commission has proposed setting up of a mission, headed by the prime minister to transform the entire scenario of science education and research in the country. Similarly, the commission has also suggested that a 'science and mathematics mission' be constituted with a team of 40-50 'brightest of the bright' Indian scientists and mathematicians below the age of 45 years. Such an initiative would be launched across the country covering every school, college, university and institution.

Science is an intellectual nursery for the next generation scientists and technologists. For later training in science, our school students need a foundation of good understanding, something well learnt and comprehended as clear knowledge. Unfortunately, our system of teaching and learning in science has almost remained the same as it was almost a century ago. Teachers are still clinging to the older ways of looking at science as a collection of facts, concepts and principles. This mind-set of teachers has failed to generate a spark of enthusiasm for science in the learners. The textbooks are full of dead bits of information and closed conclusions. They lack tentativity and experimental approach which is the real spirit and nature of science. The classrooms have been reduced into 'lesson hearing rooms' where the students are told about the subject matter and expected to commit it to memory. Thus, the authoritarian and tradition bound methods have reduced most of the science teaching to mere 'mind filling' in place of 'mind making'.

The main drawback of science teaching in our educational institutions is that instead of striking a balance between content and method or product and process, we have been emphasizing all through these years the knowledge or 'product' aspect of science. The 'Process' aspect has been relegated to background. This misplaced emphasis has equated study of science to a 'stamp, collection of facts' and a 'game of getting an exact answer'. Our children and youth have become passive consumers of scientific facts and concepts, evading the process of inquiry that is necessary to make them active investigators. In the teachers training institutions, the prospective teachers are seen militating against one of the fundamental principles of human growth and development as they tend to reward unquestioning and conformist behaviour of the learners. This type of restrictive practice followed by the teacher stifles creative expression and disparage the experimental mind.

To ameliorate teaching and learning of science in the schools and colleges, the first step required to be taken immediately is to rejuvenate the State Institutes of Science Education existing in all the states. The District Institutes of

Education and Training should also be asked to shoulder the responsibility of improving science education in the primary schools. By laying a firm foundation of science education in the primary schools, we can hope to build a better superstructure of science in the country. I think the best way to raise the quality of science teaching and learning is to relate classroom learning with the local environment and to use it as a laboratory. For example, in rural areas, a science teacher can teach a score of scientific concepts and principles by demonstrating to the students the structure and function of various parts of bullock cart, tractor and bicycle. The teacher's training institutions can be engaged in preparing 'teacher proof' instructional material to compensate and overcome the crisis of non-availability of well prepared science teachers in rural and tribal areas. College and university teachers can also be invited to participate in the project. NCTE and NCERT, being at the helm of affair of teachers' education, can be entrusted to design a national programme for preparing better and effective teachers of science.

# 30

# Taboo on Tenderness in Science Teaching

Well known human psychologist A.H. Maslow has revolutionary views on science teaching. He is of the opinion that science has come to mean primarily: practice, caution, carefulness, slowness and the art of not making mistakes rather than courage, daring, taking big chances and gambling everything on a single throw. Students are made to behave like military police, and not as commando raiders. Our orthodox conception of science (as mechanistic and a-human) seems to him one local manifestation or expression of the larger more inclusive 'weltanschauung' of mechanistic dehumanization of which it is a part.

Student is rewarded only for being patient, cautious, stubborn, controlled, mcticulous, suspicious, orderly, neat and the like. "Some effort is made to train out of him his wilderness his conventionality, his rebelliousness against his elders, his poetic and aesthetic qualities, his gaity, his 'B-humour', his craziness, his impulsiveness, his feminine qualities, his mystical impulses and much more besides". This is why many many brilliant students drop out of science. They are asked to give up too much of their human nature, too many of the rewards of living, and even some of the main values that led them to think of science in the first place. In effect, they are asked, like monks, to renounce some very precious aspects of the world. And this is doubly true of just those students who are most likely to be creative ones, the innovators.

The science teachers, very frequently adhere to the "nothing-but-attitude" in the teaching of science. They teach that "a human being is really nothing but $100 worth chemicals", or a rainbow is nothing but the scattering of white light into colours by droplets acting like prisms. This is a sort of devaluation of child's experience. Teachers should not pose a threat to everything that the students, hold marvelous, beautiful, valuable, sacred and awe-inspiring. Otherwise, the picture of life in the minds of science students would be bleak, cold and mechanical. Science should get rid of this quite unnecessary 'taboo on tenderness'. So for as science is considered, the self-actualizing healthy people teach us, says Maslow, that "there is no real opposition between caution and courage, between vigour and speculation, between tough mindedness and tender mindedness. These are all human qualities, and they are all useful in science."

# 31

# Spiritual Leadership: Why and What?

**Introduction: The Leadership Scenario in the Country**

In our country most of the institutions and organizations are under-led. In the political arena we don't find single 'statesman' or a great leader who is acceptable throughout the length and breadth of the country. There is a crowd of pigmy politicians who even don't know the history, geography and astronomy of the country. We have professional economists at the helm of affair of the nation, but the economic reforms initiated in the year 1991, could not acquire a 'human face' till today. The rabit of reforms has first turned into a turtle and then into a rock. Our leaders have failed to significantly reduce the level of poverty and illiteracy. Recently, in the report of a commission, headed by Arjun Sengupta, it has been revealed that we have stunning 77% people, who live below the poverty line. Dr. Manmohan Singh's sensitivity remains confined to shedding invisible tears in the form of regrets and self-pity. But the people of India know that lamentation and condolences, over a trail of suicides in the farmer's community, can not grow crops and mitigate the woes of the marginal farmers.

We have a large number of 'Merchants of Venice', presiding over the institutions of higher learning, who are mercilessly fleecing the 'pound of flesh' in the form of high fees charged from the students without imparting quality education to them. It is rather difficult to name a vice-chancellor in the country whose university is completely free from chaos, crisis and corruption. Thus, we witness that there is an almost total collapse of 'leadership' in almost, all walks of life. A few years ago, Mr. Lee, the former prime minister of Singapore visited India. Having gained information from the people and newspapers about lack of social discipline, chaotic conditions in the cities and astounding political confusion, he humorously implored the then prime minister to give India to Singapore on lease for two-three years, to set things right and to ensure excellent functioning of the country.

### The Idea of Leadership

Leadership or leaders can not be bought or barrowed because institutions and organizations of a country are rooted in its culture and ethos. Leaders borrowed from a foreign country do not fit well like borrowed garments, in the host country. Leaders like plants should grow in the soil, sunshine and moisture of the organization. They have to be groomed by collaborative and interactive transactions and interventions taking place between the leaders and their fellow workers. An ideal and democratic course would be to derive leadership from the co-workers. It should be the privilege of the colleagues to pick up one of them to take up the responsibility of leading them. A leader can be identified on the basis of his or her urge and drive to take initiative and responsibility to promote team work. To get accepted as a leader, an individual is required to have an overwhelming passion for novelty, change and excellence. Institutions of higher education are expected to produce leaders who can provide leadership in various walks of life in the country.

A true leader, says C.J. Jung, "is always led". Perhaps, Jung means here a symbiotic relationship between the leader and his fellow workers. A leader has to be a competent and caring person who is normally prepared to share his views and ideas with his colleagues. George Bernard Shaw has rightly said that "if you have an idea, and I have an idea, and we exchange these ideas, then each of us will have two ideas". Thus, the leaders shape and get shaped during the process of shaping others. In its essence, the job of a leader is very much similar to that of an educator so far as the objective of unfolding the potential of coworkers and mobilization of their energy and talent is concerned.

Revolutionary leader manager Jack Welch held the view that "great people, no great strategies, are what made it all work...... The notion of strategy is not a lengthy action plan, but the evolution of a central idea through continually changing circumstances. While information will be made available as never before, it will always be human judgement that will make the organization go..... So far as the "human element" (or human resources element) is concerned, we need to increasingly create an atmosphere where people dare to try new things - where people feel assured in knowing that only the limits of their creativity and drive, their own standards of personal excellence, will be the ceiling on how far and how fast they move.. ..When we talk about quality and excellence, we mean creating an atmosphere where every individual across the whole company (or organization) is striving to be proud of every product and service we provide. It means all of the employs stretching beyond our limits to be, in some cases, better than we thought we could be".

**Business Leadership**

In the book named: *Naked Conversations* (2006), the authors, Robert Scoble and Shel Isael have capsuled the theme of the book as : *How blogs are changing the way business talk with customers.* While elaborating their ideas they say: "We live in a time when most people don't trust big companies. Headlines gush with tales of mal-feasance, abuse and old-fashioned plunder, but that is just a part of the problem. There is general perception that large companies are run by slick lawyers and book fixing accountants who oversea armies of obedient, drove-like employees. Companies are perceived as monoliths without souls". I think at present the world is too much with the C.E.O.'s and managers of corporations as the great poet William Wordsworth has pointed out long ago:

"The world is too much with us;
Late and soon,
Getting and spending, we lay waste our powers;
Little we see in nature that is ours;
We have given our hearts away, a sordid boon".

Similarly, the following proverb sharply summarizes the adverse effect of the race for money:

"Only when the last tree has died and the last river been poisoned, will we realize we can not eat money" ?

The young managers are very much materialized in their outlook and action. The temptation that propels most of them to work is largely that of profit and power. Managers or business leaders are rarely educated and trained to go beyond the silvery sheen of pay-packages and advocacy for consumerism. Most of the B-schools are producing myopic managers. They hardly have holistic, broad and empathic vision. The mushrooming new breed of managers hold ideas and approaches which don't have the strength to mitigate the misery of marginalized and destitute people. Renowned management Guru C.K. Prahalad has been selling an idea to raise the appetite for consumption, of the poorest of the poor, so that they can buy the products marketed by the multinationals. This is something like asking bald-headed people to purchase American combs, and the illiterates to have expensive French fountain pens. I suppose, such an advocacy will be justified if the bald-headed persons are enabled to grow hair on their heads, and the illiterates to acquire requisite literacy. Without responding to fulfill their basic needs, inducing them to consume redundant or unnecessary products would amount to misleading them to drain out their scarce and negligible resources. A spiritualized leader or management specialist will, first of all, work with the poverty stricken people to arrive at an accurate diagnosis, and then he would help them to create resources to satisfy their basic minimum needs. He will desist himself from putting cart before the horse. How long will the corporators shirk from the social responsibility to genuinely work for mitigating the miseries of the disadvantaged people.

**Spirituality and Leadership**

Human beings are spiritual beings having physical experience, and an ability to connect with the common men. Deepak Chopra looks at creativity and spirituality as highly correlated concepts. He thinks that creativity directed outside is science and technology, while creativity directed inside is spirituality. Paul Burton thinks that spirituality is a beautiful combination of conscience and compassion. Satchel Paige illustrates the idea of spirituality through the following situational examples: "Work like you don't need money; love like your heart has never been broken, and dance as if no one is watching".

Infact, spirituality is made up of inner life. It is our true essence and that part of life which relates to our soul. It is the foundation of our most closely held values, the seat of our trust and hope. Spirituality brings purpose and meaning to life, and as we develop it, we grow in wisdom, love and empathy. We begin to experience a sense of connection to all of life, and a deep reverence for the things divine. Spirituality calls a human being to a life of trust and service. When our spirituality in nurtured and vibrant, we feel connected. This connection is both a sense of relationship to the creator, as well as a relationship to all people and the Mother Earth.

Spirituality takes us beyond our ego-centred lives by expanding our hearts with compassion towards all. Spirituality involves a reverent attitude to all things because it awakens us to a divine presence in all things (ईशा वास्यं इदं सर्वम् ). In this way of seeing and being, all things and persons are interconnected and inter dependent: "I in you and you in me". Religion and spirituality are related and intertwined, but they are not the same. Religion serves us best, when devoid of narrowness and dogma, and then it acts as a vehicle to nourish and develop our spirituality.

Spiritualization of leaders will make them 'servant-leaders', and not the master ones. Surely, they will be required to resist all attempts to domesticate people around them, so that the weak are not made to submit to the wishes of the strong and powerful. Spiritualized leaders are liberated persons and they act as liberating or emancipating agents in the sphere of their work and influence. They create those conditions in the organization in which the fellow workers can voluntarily participate, put questions and give expression to their ideas. The spiritual leader also aims at imbibing and spreading the perennial message delivered by Lord Krishna that "Karma alone is man's guru, nothing but Karma alone is his God or 'Ishwara': "Karmeva gururishwara" (कर्मैव गुरूरीश्वरः). The true human being or spiritual leader is inspired by the idea of 'Sthitapragya' (स्थितप्रज्ञ) and try to stabilize his mind and intellect. He works with the resolve to be guided by the dictum : "आत्मनो मोक्षार्थम् जगद्हितायच" (working for liberation of self and good of all).

Spiritual leaders have the responsibility to convert leadership into a dynamic relationship, based on mutual influence and common purpose, between leaders and co-workers, in which both are moved to higher levels of motivation and moral development as they effect a real intended change. Influence come from integrity. Integrity means doing what you say. Integrity gives you trust and credibility without which you can have no influence. There is a dignity in contributing to another person's freedom. There is a sense of significance and a feeling of accomplishment when you know that you have played a small part in lightening the load of a colleague, who is overwhelmed. The acts of 'servanthood' are dignifying, not demeaning. The focus is on seeing the legitimate wants and needs of the people, they are about, even if this involves some pain and self-sacrifice. A spiritualized leader needs to display a cohesive fusion of brain, heart and soul.

# Index

U